"Our hope is that, as your faith continues to grow, our sphere...will greatly expand, so that we can preach the gospel in the regions beyond you."

2 Corinthians 10:15-16 (NIV)

BEYOND

A VISION FOR TEN CITIES

DAVID CANNISTRACI

CONTENTS

Our vision is a compassionate response to the pain and brokenness of people. Like Jesus, we must hear the cry of the oppressed that echoes from beyond our immediate circumstances.

The works of darkness in people's lives must be challenged. Like Jesus, we are called to overcome the obstacles before us, get engaged, and make a difference in people's lives.

An encounter with the Holy Spirit clarified His surprising purpose for our ministry and is stretching us into a larger vision than we had previously imagined.

Our vision, built on a passion for cities, comes from the Lord. As we commit to reaching cities, God will bless us and expand our reach.

DEDICATION

This book is dedicated to Team GateWay—the hundreds of men, women, young people, and children who serve in the many ministries of GateWay City Church. Service is the power plant of our church community. Nothing gets accomplished without it, and it's always been those who understand this who have moved our mission forward. We simply would not exist apart from the deep generosity and faithful service of our volunteer set-up people, hospitality teams, baristas, small group leaders, cleaners, teachers, nursery attendants, interns, elders, board members, ushers, greeters, musicians, security people, intercessors, creative people, sound and media people, and... shall I go on?

Please insert your name right here, and understand this: You are among the best people I've ever known.

> *"For God is not unjust to forget your work and labor of love which you have shown toward His name, in that you have ministered to the saints, and do minister."*
> *Hebrews 6:10*

GRATITUDE

It takes a team to make the important things in life happen. Even a small book like this required the time, support, and energy of a big group. I want to thank each and every one of them.

Debbie Pangborn has transcribed scores of my audio messages, including some that were relied on for this work. She is one of the most cheerful people I know! Amy Fyfe was my editor and really helped me organize the content and flow of ideas. She has mad grammatical skills (she probably fixed this very sentence!), and I'd still be working on it if it weren't for her help. GateWay's pastoral team helped me think through the questions and needs of our readers, and our creative team helped me come up with the title. Hans Bennewitz made the cover and interior look amazing. I truly appreciate each of these partners and what they brought to the project.

Designing our organization and carrying out multisite ministry across distant cities also takes teamwork. Our founding pastor, executive team, staff members, campus pastors, board members, and my wife Kathy have all faithfully partnered with me to make bring this vision to a reality. I can't imagine trying to do multisite ministry without the advice and experience of my ministry coach, Pastor Frank Damazio, and my good friends Pastor Derrill Corbin and Pastor Mel Mullen.

Finally, nothing in my life would work without the daily help of the Holy Spirit. Those are not empty words—they are my testimony. That I have so often felt inadequate would be no surprise. Yet I have discovered that there is never a challenge so great, or a personal weakness so acute that the Helper has not been sufficient to see me through. In every way, I am most grateful for Him.

INTRODUCTION

Every time I teach the Word of God, I trust in my heart that it is a word from heaven. The truths I'm about to share with you, though, are of a particularly great importance, because they came out of a memorable encounter that I had with the Holy Spirit. I don't want you to get the wrong idea—I'm not a super-spiritual person. I am a normal person who believes that the Spirit of God really does intersect with our physical world. He speaks, He inspires, and He impresses. He reveals the things that we need to know.

The Bible is filled with examples of people encountering God, and in that process they discover their calling. I want to share with you a specific calling I have heard deep in my heart—a calling that can inspire anyone, especially those in our GateWay City Church family.

This is the story behind BEYOND: A Vision for Ten Cities. It is the blueprint of our future, and the fuel for a ministry together that is beyond, more fruitful, more significant, and more effective at reaching people for Christ than we ever imagined.

In this book, we will come to face to face with the needs of lost people. We will be reminded of God's great love, and we will explore our potential as the church to become an instrument of redemption in cities.

We begin in a faraway place at another time, with a dramatic story that reveals how a broken life can be transformed through an encounter with Jesus and how that life can be used to touch cities. Come with me to a place beyond the comfort and familiarity of our lives. Come with me to the Land of the Gadarenes.

THE CRY OF THE OPPRESSED

DO YOU BELIEVE IT IS POSSIBLE FOR PEOPLE TO CHANGE?

In our modern culture, superficial change is easy and everywhere. You can dye your hair, whiten your teeth, tighten your face, a little nip and tuck, suck a little excess fat, you name it!

But what about change on a deeper level? What about the kind of change where God gets into a person's life and radically alters his or her interior world?

Yes, people can and do change inside, especially when they meet Jesus. Their lives are forever altered as a result of God's healing, delivering, and freeing power. That is what the following story is all about.

YES, PEOPLE CAN AND DO CHANGE INSIDE, ESPECIALLY WHEN THEY MEET JESUS

THE LAND OF THE GADARENES

I want to take you far from here, back in time nearly 2,000 years to a place of great darkness. Join me on a prophetic journey deep into a place called Gadara, the Land of the Gadarenes. It is there we encounter the vast brokenness of the human race. This place reveals just how lost and hopelessly far we are from God apart from Christ but also shines a light on how Jesus Christ can transform even the most tormented human life.

This story begins at Mark 4:35 and concludes at Mark 5:20:

> On the same day, when evening had come, He said to them, "Let us cross over to the other side." Now when they had left the multitude, they took Him along in the boat as He was. And other little boats were also with Him. And a great windstorm arose, and the waves beat into the boat, so that it was already filling. But He was in the stern, asleep on a pillow. And they awoke Him and said to Him, "Teacher, do You not care that we are perishing?"
>
> Then He arose and rebuked the wind, and said to the sea, "Peace, be still!" And the wind ceased and there was a great calm. But He said to them, "Why are you so fearful? How is it that you have no faith?" And they feared exceedingly, and said to one another, "Who can this be that even the wind and the sea obey Him!"
>
> Then they came to the other side of the sea, to the country of the Gadarenes. And when He had come out of the boat, immediately there met Him out of the tombs a man with an unclean spirit, who had his dwelling among the tombs; and no one could bind him, not even with chains, because he had often been bound with shackles and chains. And the chains had been pulled apart by him, and the shackles broken in pieces; neither could anyone tame him. And always, night and day, he was in the mountains and in the tombs, crying out and cutting himself with stones.
>
> When he saw Jesus from afar, he ran and worshiped Him. And he cried out with a loud voice and said, "What have I to do with You, Jesus, Son of the Most High God? I implore You by God that You do not torment me."

For He said to him, "Come out of the man, unclean spirit!" Then He asked him, "What is your name?"

And he answered, saying, "My name is Legion; for we are many." Also he begged Him earnestly that He would not send them out of the country.[1]

Now a large herd of swine was feeding there, near the mountains, so all the demons begged Him, saying, "Send us into the swine, that we may enter them." And at once Jesus[c] gave them permission. Then the unclean spirits went out and entered into the swine (there were about two thousand); and the herd ran violently down the steep place into the sea, and drowned in the sea.

So those who fed the swine fled, and they told it in the city and in the country. And they went out to see what it was that had happened. Then they came to Jesus, and saw the one who had been demon-possessed and had the legion, sitting and clothed and in his right mind. And they were afraid. And those who saw it told them how it happened to him who had been demon-possessed, and about the swine. Then they began to plead with Him to depart from their region.

And when He got into the boat, he who had been de-mon-possessed begged Him that he might be with Him. However, Jesus did not permit him, but said to him, "Go home to your friends, and tell them what great things the Lord has done for you, and how He has had compassion on you." And he departed and began to proclaim in Decapolis[2] all that Jesus had done for him; and all marveled. (NKJV)

---

1. (This is a very interesting statement, and if you've ever studied territorial spirits, you'll understand that these demons did not want to be reassigned to another territory. They had an assignment in the Land of the Gadarenes and did not want that work interrupted.)

2. Decapolis means "ten cities", which we later expand upon.

In the region of the Sea of Galilee, peaceful Jewish towns dotted the sunny shores of this beautifully tranquil land, alongside an impressive inland sea of fresh water overflowing with abundant fish. Crossing the Sea of Galilee toward the opposite shore brought one into the Land of the Gadarenes, and it is there the apostles and Jesus traveled.

Compared to the Jewish land just across the Galilee, this was a strange territory, full of idols and pagan cults. Close to where this miraculous deliverance took place was a pagan temple to the god Zeus (or Baal as he was known in Israel). Local worshipers would take pigs they were raising, slit the animals' throats, and offer them as a sacrifice to the false gods at that temple.

The history of this land sheds light on our story. The Land of the Gadarenes drew its name from the tribe of Gad. In the Old Testament, when Joshua led the twelve tribes of Israel up to the Jordan to take the promised land, the tribe of Gad was assigned the lush portion of northern land on the east side of the Jordan. Initially the tribe would not have crossed over the Jordan; however, they did so because Joshua required them to fight the enemies of God and take all of the land that God was giving to the Israelites. All this had to be completed before they could then cross back over onto the far side of the Jordan and settle in the land of Gad as their home.

Gad means "troop," so it is not surprising that they were a warrior tribe, valiantly fighting the battles of the Lord before they settled back on their chosen side of the river. When they finished their mission, this territory, far from the other tribes, became known as the Land of the Gadarenes.

In Joshua 22, we read how the elders of the tribe of Gad came together with the elders of Reuben and the half-tribe of Manasseh, who were also on that side of the Jordan. At their meeting, they created a "witness altar"—a memorial altar that was erected because the tribe of Gad was so far away from the place of worship at Shiloh, where the Ark of the Covenant (the Ark of God's presence) was placed. Because they were so removed, they set up their own altar so that the people of Gad would not be cut off from the spiritual life of Israel. It was a reminder of their values and connection to their faith.

The other tribes misunderstood Gad's bid to build the altar, saying, "What do you think you are doing, setting up an altar here! Do you intend to worship a false god?"

The elders of Gad responded, "Never! It's just that we're so far away! We don't want ourselves or our children to forget that we also are a part of the life of Israel and that God has also given us this land."

This calmed the debate, and the people of Gad began their lives serving the Lord in their own country. But that distance which had been such a concern to the tribal elders of Gad did indeed end up becoming a problem. The physical space that kept them so far from the Ark and the presence of God in Shiloh eventually turned into a vast spiritual distance.

Because the law required all males over twenty to go up to Shiloh three times a year, over time, that gap made staying connected to the presence of God more and more challenging. So, imagine this scenario: wherever your tribal land in Israel is

---

THE PHYSICAL SPACE THAT KEPT THEM SO FAR FROM THE ARK AND THE PRESENCE OF GOD IN SHILOH EVENTUALLY TURNED INTO A VAST SPIRITUAL DISTANCE.

---

located, you must journey to Shiloh (later it was to Jerusalem) three times a year to bring your offerings and engage in religious feasts. This was a long journey, especially for the distant tribe of Gad, taking a week or more to complete when coming from the Land of the Gadarenes.

All the males in the Israelite nation had to leave their jobs, families, crops, livestock, and farms. They had to drop everything and make a long journey all the way to Shiloh with their tithes and sacrifices; they would participate in the celebrations and then have to travel all the way back home. Even though coming together to worship in community was a pleasant experience, it was also a hardship. When settling into their land, the tribe of Gad had feared that over time Shiloh was so far away that they might lose their connection with God, and sadly, that is exactly what happened.

Despite every warning to the Tribe of Gad, this land that had once been granted by God as a possession to this Israelite tribe had become a very dark place. By the time Jesus arrived there, a possessed man had identified himself to Jesus by stating, "We are Legion"; a Roman legion was up to six-thousand strong, well-organized soldiers. The land of the Gadarenes was probably one of the few places in the world that a man could be infested with six-thousand demons.

How does the land that God gave as a promise to the tribe of Gad become filled with demons, darkness, and the sacrificing of unclean animals to idols and false gods? How does good Jewish territory become so infested with evil?

Spiritual darkness can get attached to regions and to land where spirits will seek to operate and manifest. Hundreds of years after the Tribe of Gad first possessed it, this land, far from the presence of God had become the perfect atmosphere for spiritual oppression.

PORTRAIT OF PAIN

Jesus began His ministry among both the Jews and the Gentiles by casting out demons. But never anywhere else in Scripture do we see that that one person could have had thousands of demons like this man did. Perhaps all the demons encountered in Jesus' ministry combined wouldn't have been six-thousand!

Here lived a man so possessed and so hopeless that he encased perhaps the greatest spiritual battle that Jesus encountered in His entire ministry.

We know five shocking facts about this man and the extent of his oppression:

NO ONE COULD TAME HIM

He couldn't be chained and he couldn't be tamed. This is an interesting phrase because you don't typically tame men; you tame wild animals. Yet, here's a man with thousands of demons whom no one can calm; he lived naked, cutting himself day and night, and constantly crying out in the mountains and hills. The inference is that he had become like an animal and had even lost the appearance of a normal human. The only thing you could do with somebody like that was try to chain and tame him, but it couldn't be done. The chains served only as tormenting fetters symbolizing his tragic condition.

HE LIVED AMONG THE TOMBS

Tombs are morbid places of death and loss. They are nothing but a constant reminder of brokenness, death, disease, as well as dreams and lives that are cut short. This was his chosen dwelling place, likely because the demons within him felt comfortable in that atmosphere. To the Jews, tombs were a forbidden place of uncleanness, but to this poor man, it became home.

HERE LIVED A MAN SO POSSESSED AND SO HOPELESS THAT HE ENCASED PERHAPS THE GREATEST SPIRITUAL BATTLE THAT JESUS ENCOUNTERED IN HIS ENTIRE MINISTRY.

HE WAS SELF-DESTRUCTIVE

This is one of the most pitiful aspects of this story. The Bible tells us that he could not stop cutting himself with stones.

I remember a mentally tormented man in our church years ago who could not stop pulling his hair; I will never forget his agony. He was so tormented with anxiety that he had great patches of hair missing from his head. Similarly, the possessed man Jesus encountered obsessively cut himself.

DAY AND NIGHT, THIS MAN WAS CUTTING HIMSELF TO MASK A DEEP LEVEL OF PAIN IN HIS SOUL.

You can't imagine the appearance of this man. Some of his wounds were fresh, and some of his skin was scarred from years and years of self-abuse. When people are in so much emotional and psychological pain that they would rather suffer a flesh wound than deal with the pain in their hearts, it is because the internal distress is so great that the distraction of a new wound seems like a relief. Day and night, this man was cutting himself to mask a deep level of pain in his soul.

HE WAS UNCOVERED

Neither cared for nor protected by those around him, this man had been abandoned to his demons for some time. He would remain naked and tortured in squalor.

Similarly, there are so many uncovered and unprotected people in our world today. Where are the parents of children who are abandoned? Where are the fathers who should be protecting their children from pornography, sex trafficking, and the like?

There are so many uncovered and unprotected people in our culture with no one to fight for them, no one to treasure them, and no one to defend them. Like the unclothed state of this possessed man, there is a spiritual nakedness within our culture that should break our hearts.

HE WAS UTTERLY TORMENTED

Why would Jesus leave the quiet serenity of a lazy fishing town in His beautiful sun-soaked home in Capernaum, where life was good, miracles and healings were taking place, and His ministry was expanding? He chose to leave His safe Jewish community to cross over twelve miles of inland sea to enter into a place brimming with darkness, demons, pagan worship, and oppression. But why in the world would He do it?

To say that the demon-possessed man was mentally ill falls a thousand times short of the reality of his situation. The Bible says that he was tormented by his demons. He was in such pain that he cried out day and night. I believe Jesus both physically and spiritually heard that cry, just as He hears the cry of every broken heart.

WHAT DID JESUS HEAR?

If you visit Galilee, when the water is still with a gentle breeze blowing in the right direction, it is said that you can hear sounds from across the sea. The Bible says that on a specific day Jesus said to His disciples, "Let us cross over." He had spent the previous night in prayer in the mountains. So, could it be that when Jesus was up on a mountain praying in the stillness of the night, He heard the sound of this man's tormented cry? Whether it was His natural ear or His spiritual ear, Jesus was connecting with the desperate wailing of a man in complete agony.

I cannot impersonate the cry of a man filled with six thousand demons. The volume of it, the hopelessness of it, the desperation of it! It was a cry that came from beyond—a cry for change. This cry is what influenced Jesus to tell His disciples the next day, "Let's go beyond. There's oppression in the Land of the Gadarenes." May that cry touch us and move us into the beyond of broken lives!

As we read the story from Mark 4 and 5, we find that Jesus did indeed cross over. He came to encounter this poor, oppressed man, and confront the demonic spirits that were holding him captive. He was instantly set free and restored to his right mind.

He had commanded them, "Come out of him, you unclean spirits!" Because they had a job to do, an assignment in that region, they begged of Him, "Please don't send us out of this area!" Sensing that their time remaining in this man was coming to a rapid end, they tried to negotiate a deal with Jesus: "Look, we know You're going to cast us out, but don't throw us into the lake of fire! Don't throw us into the abyss! Can we please go into the pigs instead?"

I can just see Jesus pulling His beard, laughing and thinking, "This is perfect! Go to the pigs where you belong!" He gave them permission to go, and so they did. Ironically, these pigs, now freshly filled with demonic spirits, ran screaming and plunging to their deaths off a cliff into the Sea of Galilee. It almost makes you feel sorry for the pigs!

The possessed man fell down worshiping at the feet of Jesus. And notice this man's first instinct after he had been gloriously set free. He said, "Lord, I want to follow you. Can I join You in ministry?"

Jesus knew he was not yet ready for full-time ministry. So, He gave him an assignment which he could and did carry out beautifully. Jesus instructed, "Go home and tell people how the Lord has had compassion on you and how God has set you free." The man did as he was told.

Now that he was totally restored, it must have been amazing to sit in his presence and hear his story and see his scars, to understand what he had been through and how Jesus Christ had so powerfully restored him. Jesus had broken the enemy's assignment in this land of tremendous spiritual oppression. What an amazing story!

But make careful note how our story ends, because it relates to our calling: the Bible says that this man gave his testimony all throughout Decapolis, the ten Roman Cities on that side of the sea that have become so intrinsic to our vision today. He began to be famous in that area for telling everyone what Jesus had done for him!

ENTERING IN TO THE CALL

You and I have the same calling to cross over into the beyond and change lives just as Jesus did. We have that same responsibility because our own lives have been changed. It is important that we give the glory to God for this. We cannot just say, "Well, I freed myself. Yes, I was able to overcome my fears and accomplish all these great things myself." We know that this is not the case!

JESUS HAD BROKEN THE ENEMY'S ASSIGNMENT IN THIS LAND OF TREMENDOUS SPIRITUAL OPPRESSION.

Jesus Christ is the Savior! He is the healer! He is the one who has taught us to think, taught us to love, and taught us how to sleep peacefully at night. Like the demoniac from Gadara, the Lord has set us free, and, therefore, we have the responsibility and privilege to lead others to their deliverance in Him. The Gadarene man entered into his calling in the region of the Ten Cities because he was passionate about making others aware of what God had done. Can we do any less?

CONCLUSION

Can we hear the cries for change coming from those around us? Have you and I become so busy that we can't hear the cries of suffering people beyond our safe and comfortable existence? If so, we need to wake up and follow Jesus beyond the comfort of our present life—beyond the raging storms and our fear of the unknown—into the Land of the Gadarenes where God will demonstrate His miraculous power to heal a broken life.

**CAN WE HEAR THE CRIES FOR CHANGE
COMING FROM THOSE AROUND US?**

ANOINTED TO INTERFERE

I'm fascinated with the miraculous story of the Gadarene because it demonstrates that true ministry is about interference. Real ministry is getting involved with something that isn't our business but God has made our business. We live in a world that would love nothing more than if we would just have nice Sunday services separate from the darkness in the world. It is impressed upon the Christian community that it would be best if we would pray and sing our songs about heaven, and then go into our neighborhoods silent, saying and doing absolutely nothing; we must never go beyond. Tragically, sometimes we settle for that.

But, you see, Jesus has to disturb the status quo. He loves to interfere. He said, "The Spirit of the Lord is upon me, for He has anointed me to bring good news to the poor" (Luke 4:18, NLT). There comes a time when God rises up and He says, "Right now! That captivity will be broken, the blind will see, and the oppressed will be set free. This is the time that the Lord's favor has come." I believe that He is saying that now. It is the time for something beyond the status quo to happen in our ministries and churches.

A VISION FOR TEN CITIES

Jesus got involved with human suffering. Similarly, whatever we do in ministry is our way of interfering with the injustice, pain, and suffering that the enemy has planned for people. We cannot ignore that that is his ultimate plan, and we must acknowledge the reality that, unopposed, he will succeed. Through His example, Jesus is showing us that we should live our faith out before the world and, in doing so, have an incredibly powerful impact. He wants us to follow Him as He crosses over and goes beyond to interrupt the enemy's unbridled oppression of people.

HE WANTS US TO FOLLOW HIM AS HE CROSSES OVER AND GOES BEYOND TO INTERRUPT THE ENEMY'S UNBRIDLED OPPRESSION OF PEOPLE.

The story in Mark reflects this idea of powerful faith perfectly. Jesus crossed a great geographic barrier (the Sea of Galilee), pressing even through a storm that rose up against Him, and when He eventually came to the shore, the first thing that occurred was demons started speaking out of a possessed man.

They implored Jesus, "Why must you interfere with what's happening here? We beg you, don't torment us, don't disrupt our work, and don't send us away!" The enemy wants to stay in a position of control, and he's afraid that somebody who is anointed will come and break his ability to bind and oppress people. Six-thousand demons screamed out, "Why are you interfering?!"

Jesus did what He did because the very essence of the presence of God is interference with darkness.

By the end of the story, the man from Gadara is totally restored and in his right mind. No longer tormented, he is clothed, calm, safe, having experienced a radical miracle! The people of the

**JESUS DID WHAT HE DID BECAUSE THE VERY ESSENCE OF
THE PRESENCE OF GOD IS INTERFERENCE WITH DARKNESS.**

area who witnessed this event turned to Jesus and, surprisingly enough said, "Please leave us now." Why?

When we talk about territorial spirits and the iniquity that can capture a land, what's a more effective method of capture for a region than just the belief that things should just remain as they are? It's when people feel they don't need change and don't want change that territorial strongholds are established. The saddest thing about being captive for so long is that it often causes people to say, "I really don't want to be free."

Darkness prefers the status-quo. Just leave everything as it is. That mindset can get into me and it can get into you. We don't want to be interrupted or inconvenienced, and we don't want God to show up and mess up our predictable way of life, even if it torments us.

Apathy is the one of the hallmarks of darkness. I've also noticed that Jesus actually prefers change, especially when people are hurting, especially when there are victims, and especially where there's pain. It's the character of His anointing to interrupt and change things. He wants us to go beyond.

HE HEARS THE CRY
I don't know if you hear it, but there's a cry in your community, there's a cry in America, there's a cry in the nations! All around us people are living in the Land of the Gadarenes. They're young, they're old, they're our neighbors, they're our coworkers, they are gay, they are straight, they are black, they are white, they're in our churches, and they're in our schools. They are everywhere, and they are crying out because of their oppression.

They live in the homeless shelter and at the country club. They are cutters, and they are people who look perfectly happy on the outside yet are secretly overwhelmed with depression. Filled with pain, they cry out from the Land of the Gadarenes. You don't have to go far to notice the oppression, the hurt, and the bondage. If we'll open our spiritual ears, we cannot avoid hearing their cry.

Here's a word for us from Psalm 12:5, and if you're interested in justice ministry, please take special note of this because this has become prophetic to me.

IF WE'LL OPEN OUR SPIRITUAL EARS, WE CANNOT AVOID HEARING THEIR CRY.

The Lord replies, "I have seen the violence done to the helpless and I have heard the groans of the poor. Now I will rise up to rescue them as they have longed for Me to do." (NLT)

GOD HEARS THE CRY FOR CHANGE!

The children of Israel cried out from the oppression of their Egyptian slavery for hundreds of years, yet didn't hear a word from God, never had a prophet, and their situation continued to grow worse. Then one day a man named Moses was in the wilderness when he turned aside and saw a bush engulfed in flame that did not burn! And out of that bush came a voice; it was God saying, "I have heard the cry of the children of Israel, and I'm sending you to them."

Moses, completely overcome, replied, "You've got the wrong guy! You probably meant this message for somebody else. I don't have the gift of speaking. What if the Israelites don't believe me? And who are you, by the way?"

But God, not to be pushed aside, answered, "I am sending you. I have chosen who I have chosen. Do not try to escape this call or resist me."

Just as Moses was chosen and equipped by God to go beyond, so also is God calling and equipping us. We don't have the excuse of saying, "Well, that's what Jesus or Moses did, but I don't do that." You do not have that reason because the same Holy Spirit that is in Jesus is in you. If you're born again and if you've received Christ, you have the Holy Spirit.

WHEN YOU JOIN JESUS, AND GO BEYOND
The minute you decide to let God use you to interrupt darkness, everything changes. Here are five things we can expect when we go beyond with Jesus to interfere with the works of the enemy.

STORMS WILL ARISE
Storms will arise in the Land of the Gadarenes. If you set off in a direction of helping those who are hurting, you are going to end up face first in a storm just like Jesus did. So don't be surprised and think, "Well, this should have been easy! I thought I would cruise over on a pleasure craft into the land of the Gadarenes where there would be ponies and rainbows to greet me on the shore."

Even Jesus didn't have that kind of experience! When Jesus crossed over the Sea of Galilee, a demonic storm rose up. I'm here to tell you the very moment when God is going to show up and do something great in your life a mighty storm may very well blow your way.

Instead of saying to yourself, "Well, I must be doing something wrong because all hell is breaking loose in my life," keep on heading in the direction that God leads you. Keep following Jesus because it is inevitable that storms will rise up, and many of them will be demonic. Don't you dare turn around because of a demonic storm! When you're on your assignment, you must keep pressing forward.

People all around you may be freaking out, and want you to worry with them, just like the disciples did when they complained to Jesus, "Hey! Don't you care that we're all dying? Aren't you afraid too?" Some will get mad at you for not being anxious with them, but you must maintain your composure and do as Jesus did. You can speak to that storm knowing that it's not a natural but a spiritual thing.

What did He say to the storm? "Peace!"

Suddenly it was as calm as it could be. The spiritual storm broke, and it's going to break over your life as well if you'll stand up to it. Stay the course and trust in God.

Over the years of building our church and reaching out to our city, there have been some storms. By God's grace, we have never turned around. Instead, we are choosing to trust God in the storm.

**WHEN YOU'RE ON YOUR ASSIGNMENT,
YOU MUST KEEP PRESSING FORWARD.**

THERE IS SPIRITUAL HUNGER
There is incredible spiritual hunger in the Land of the Gadarenes. As soon as Jesus' feet hit the ground, this man filled with demons ran directly toward Jesus, fell at His feet, and worshiped Him. Even six-thousand demons could not keep one hungry heart from worshiping Jesus! So compelling was Jesus, and His love so irresistible, that this man was drawn like a magnet to the presence of the Lord. He could not help but start worshiping. Perhaps this was the first time that real worship had taken place in the Land of the Gadarenes in a thousand years!

PERHAPS THIS WAS THE FIRST TIME THAT REAL WORSHIP HAD TAKEN PLACE IN THE LAND OF THE GADARENES IN A THOUSAND YEARS!

I'll tell you something about worship: it releases the power of God. This man didn't know it, but he was participating in his own deliverance because he became a worshiper, and doing that released the power of God to break the darkness of his bondage.

Worship activates the healing power of God. It activates faith and it breaks chains. We don't go to church to sing a few pretty songs and then just stop. We go to break through to the presence of God, to worship until strongholds are broken.

There is such hunger in the Land of the Gadarenes, and you and I will begin to feel something moving when the presence of Jesus shows up there.

GOD WILL DO UNUSUAL THINGS
We may have to break conventions when we come into the Land of the Gadarenes. God loves to do unusual miracles (Acts 19:11). We might have to break a few rules while we are interfering, and we might need to do things in a different way than religious people expect us to do them.

GOD LOVES TO DO UNUSUAL MIRACLES (ACTS 19:11).

For instance, as Jesus lands on the Gadarene shore soaking wet from the demonic storm, suddenly, this unknown and frightening man who lives in a tomb comes out and starts running toward Him. Yet, Jesus doesn't turn away, but walks straight toward him!

What's a nice Jewish boy doing walking straight into the midst of an unclean cemetery? Jesus didn't have a problem with unusual things. He didn't have a fear of death because He is the resurrection and the life.

As part of our mission, whether it be planting campuses, rescuing trafficked girls, helping homeless people, or working with the next generation, we should know it's not all traditional, tidy church ministry. Some of it is untraditional and some of it is unusual. But it is time that we confront the needs around us.

THE YOKE IS BROKEN

The anointing breaks the yoke in the Land of the Gadarenes. No man could tame the demoniac from Gadara; no government or psychologist, and no preacher or social worker could have done it! Only the anointing that was on Jesus' life could have broken that man free.

Nowadays, we would have probably locked that man up a long time ago and just sedated him for his own good. But it was the power of the Holy Spirit upon the life of Jesus that was able to do the job.

**LET'S TAP INTO GOD'S HEALING POWER,
AND USE IT TO REACH PEOPLE!**

In Genesis 37:25 and Jeremiah 8:22, 46:11, it talks about the "The Balm of Gilead." Gilead is the land of Gad, which means that Gilead is the Land of the Gadarenes. Out of the very place of darkness grows a plant producing a resin that is a medicinal oil! This balm of Gilead is a picture of Christ's anointing and how it will be used to heal a person's life. Therefore, there is healing medicine available even in the dark Land of the Gadarenes. Let's tap into God's healing power, and use it to reach people!

LIVES ARE TRANSFORMED

We'll see lives transformed in the Land of the Gadarenes. It doesn't matter how severe the bondage is, a life can change even in a place of total darkness. A demon-possessed man can be transformed into a man sitting clothed and in his right mind. Only Jesus can do that, because He is anointed to interfere.

As a church, our vision and culture is stated in three powerful words: "Inspiring Transformed Lives". That's what it's all about. That's why we do everything we do, and I invite you to join us in this powerful purpose.

As we bring this chapter to a close, there are three things that I must point out about this story:

SIN BRINGS BONDAGE

I don't think any of us are as frightened of our own sins as we need to be. You see, the bondage that existed in the Land of the Gadarenes was never supposed to be. This land had started as a place dedicated to God and set aside for the children of Israel. Had they kept their land clean, it would have been a virtual paradise.

How does good land become the Land of the Gadarenes? It happens when people neglect their spiritual duties. When, because of distance and difficulty, spiritual essentials like church, prayer, Scripture reading, and fellowship become inconvenient, we turn away from the presence of God. Stay connected to God's house. Stay in fellowship with God's people, no matter what.

If there is a part of your life that you are not actively welcoming the Lord into, you can be sure that that area of your life will be taken over very quickly. You will find yourself filled with oppressions and evil that you do not understand.

---

3. Restlessness is one of the primary indications of demonic oppression.

Jesus made it very clear in John 10:10 that,

> *The thief comes with the sole intention of stealing and killing and destroying. That's what the devil will do every time! But I came to bring them life and far more life than before. I'm the Good Shepherd. The Good Shepherd will give His life for the sake of the sheep. The enemy won't give his life for you but Christ has. (JBP)*

If pigs won't live in bondage, why do we? If a pig can't stand the presence of a demon and will deliberately run off a cliff to escape it, why do we tolerate the presence of evil in our own homes? Let Jesus fill the land of your heart. Don't follow the poor example of the Tribe of Gad who didn't keep their land spiritually free.

WE ARE FREE IN CHRIST
For everyone who has Christ, your story reads as follows:

> *And you were dead in the trespasses and sins in which you once walked, following the course of this world, following the prince of the power of the air, the spirit that is now at work in the sons of disobedience—among whom we all once lived in the passions of our flesh, carrying out the desires of the body and the mind, and were by nature children of wrath, like the rest of mankind. But God, being rich in mercy, because of the great love with which he loved us, even when we were dead in our trespasses, made us alive together with Christ—by grace you have been saved—and raised us up with him and seated us with him in the heavenly places in Christ Jesus. (Ephesians 2:1-6, ESV)*

LET GOD GIVE YOU PEACE, FOR HE HAS SEATED YOU IN HEAVENLY PLACES, RULING AND REIGNING WITH HIM.

Need I remind you of the position of the possessed man when he was finally healed? He was seated, finally at rest, no longer driven to constant motion, and restlessness.[3]

If you can't rest, then you are tormented. If you're always trying to prove something, always on the move, for heaven's sakes, sit for a minute! Let a right mind come. Let God give you peace, for He has seated you in heavenly places, ruling and reigning with Him.

God's love for you is so great, you have been made free in Jesus Christ.

LIVES REALLY CAN CHANGE

In the introduction to this book, we began with an important question: Can a life change? The answer is yes. At the end of the Gadarene's story, we see a man at peace. The chains that bound him were no longer a part of his identity. He's seated, he's clothed, no longer cutting himself, no longer tormented, and no longer crying out. He is finally in his right mind.

I look forward to going to heaven one day and meeting this man. I want to sit down with this person who was so hopeless and ask him, "What was it like when you heard the voice of Jesus Christ saying to the demons, 'Get out of that man!' and all the pain stopped? What was it like to feel peace for the first time?'" I remember when I first opened my own heart to Christ; it felt like the weight of a thousand sins was lifted from my shoulders. I realized that God saw me and that He loved me, and I knew I was now clean and free.

NO MATTER WHAT YOUR PROBLEMS ARE, IF YOU CRY OUT TO THE LORD, HE'LL BE YOUR DELIVERER AND YOUR HEALER.

If you're tormented, afflicted, battling addictions, or you're wrestling with depression, I want you to know that Jesus can break that and set you free. No matter what your problems are, if you cry out to the Lord, He'll be your deliverer and your healer. What a glorious Savior He is!

There comes a time where God starts raising people up to interfere because things need to change. We are in such a time, and if we can hear the cries of the oppressed desperately seeking hope, and if we really know who God is, then we'll understand the steps we must now take.

CONCLUSION
Our calling as a church is to be a part of this life-changing process. We're not called just to be changed, but we're called to go beyond and help others to experience this change as well. We are called and anointed to interfere with the enemy's works. This is an amazing calling, and it belongs to us.

ONE CHURCH, MANY CITIES

Sunday May 1, 2016 was a day that changed my life forever. It had been a very busy Sunday. I had led an early morning board meeting followed by two full services featuring a guest speaker. Within those services there had been prophetic presbytery, the installation of elders, and the ordination of six new pastors. And the day was just getting started.

After the services concluded, I took our guest speaker out for lunch before parting ways and heading home, where I had yet another board meeting by telephone for a church I help to oversee in another state. By the time that 90-minute call was completed, I was totally exhausted. I was tired and just wanted to unplug. Turning on the television sounded great! Just a few hours without ministry.

As I settled in and relaxed, an unusual word started popping into my mind. Maybe you have experienced something similar: a song gets stuck in your head, or you have a word or thought consistently recur in your mind, and your brain is just filled with it. This word kept repeating itself to me, and it took a minute for me to realize that it was the Holy Spirit speaking.

The word was "Decapolis." I paused and thought about that word. I knew it was a Bible word found in the gospels, and I knew it was a geographical location at the time of Jesus, but I couldn't say that it meant anything special to me other than the fact that it just kept repeating itself: "Decapolis". Things really came into focus when I recalled that Decapolis means "ten cities". Lord, I prayed, are you speaking to me about reaching multiple cities?

After some time, I turned off the television and began looking in my Bible to read about Decapolis. As I did so, the Holy Spirit started imparting a sense of clear vision and purpose that inspired me as never before in over 35 years of ministry. I knew that I was receiving something from God that would make the world—and my world—better, more fruitful, and more meaningful. I was then drawn to consider the following verse, which hit me like a cannon ball:

"The King said to him; because you have been faithful in a very small matter, you will have authority over TEN CITIES." (Luke 19:17, emphasis mine)

This verse is referencing the parable of the faithful steward, a story that Jesus told about the importance of faithfulness. In simple terms, Jesus is saying that ministry is not really about what you don't have; it's actually about what you choose to do with that which God has given you.

FAITHFULNESS IS THE KEY
The way to increase in the Kingdom is to stop worrying about what you don't have. Quit thinking about all the things that aren't yours and think instead on what it is you do have and in what ways you could be faithful to God with it! That is how God begins to bless and increase us.

He says to us, "Because you've been faithful in a very small thing, I am now going to increase your authority." In the parable of the faithful steward, Jesus states, "You have ruled one city and now you're going to have influence that is going to touch ten cities." He loves to increase our level of responsibility if we are faithful in doing the littlest thing correctly.

Let me tell you of how this revelation of expanding authority as a result of faithfulness has taken on a powerful prophetic meaning in my life.

A MULTISITE EXPANSION
"Decapolis"... the Holy Spirit kept saying to me, and I began to see our call to cities and why the Lord had taken us as a church to more than one city.

It began about thirty years ago. We had planted a church in the city of Santa Rosa, California. The church did very well for many years, becoming healthy and strong. Tragically, about two years before I heard the Lord say "Decapolis", the pastor at this church, Paul Miller, passed away. He was a friend of mine who had been saved at the same time that Kathy and I gave our hearts to the Lord during the Jesus Movement in the seventies. About three years previous to his passing, he became very sick and eventually lost his battle with cancer.

During his illness, the church had experienced a period of suffering and decline. Eventually they found themselves in a financial crisis that they probably would not survive. Simultaneously, my friend Paul was at death's door and his church was in jeopardy.

The Holy Spirit began speaking to me regarding that situation. After talking to our team about it, I decided that we should

ALL OVER THE WORLD, CHURCHES ARE EXPANDING INTO MULTIPLE CITIES AND MORE LOCATIONS THROUGH WHAT IS CALLED THE MULTISITE MOVEMENT.

offer to adopt the church in Santa Rosa, as they clearly were not going to make it continuing as they were. Everyone agreed, and we adopted that church in a city two hours away from our home base. For the first time in our church history, we became a multisite church. We were now one church in two cities: GateWay San Jose and GateWay Santa Rosa.

That situation is not unique. All over the world, churches are expanding into multiple cities and more locations through what is called the multisite movement. Evidence shows that tens of thousands of people are being saved through these multisite churches.

I had often wondered, would God ever direct us to become a multisite church? Would such a thing ever be in God's will for us?

I wanted to be sure that I truly heard from God on the matter. I don't want to just copy something I have seen in other churches simply because it worked for them. So, we as a leadership team put this new multisite concept before the Lord.

Now, suddenly, through this unexpected circumstance, we became a multisite church. That was not the way I had imagined we would become multisite—during the loss of my friend—but that is how it happened. However, I am pleased to report that the church in Santa Rosa is doing very well, growing and becoming stronger every day.

The next step in our Decapolis journey picks up just a year later with a church in Clovis, CA, pastored by Sam and Kim Beckworth, with whom we have been connecting for seven years. They were known as Faith Summit Church of Clovis.

One day, Pastor Sam came to me and said, "I've been watching what you've done with Santa Rosa, and I was wondering, What would it look like if we became part of your church? What if we weren't Faith Summit Church anymore, and instead we became GateWay Clovis?"

Honestly, my first thought was...oh boy! This is not how I was expecting this to go. Another church more than two hours away. Will I have enough time? How will this work?

We often forget that God does things we consider unusual, and He leads us by way of seemingly strange methods. Despite my initial preconceptions about church expansion, we were now considering a third campus some distance away from the other two.

After a great deal of talking with our team, and a massive amount of prayer, I felt that we needed to take the step to receive Faith Summit as a part of our church. In August of 2016, we became one church in three locations. Since that time, we have further added GateWay Modesto (June 2017) and as of the date of this writing, are aggressively planning for several additional locations in cities that need the Lord, including Phoenix, Arizona (2019).

UNDERSTANDING DECAPOLIS
So what does this all have to do with the word "Decapolis"?

As I studied, I remembered what I had been taught in Bible School, which was that Decapolis was a colony of ten cities under the umbrella of Rome near Israel, yet was very different from Israel. So, geographically, you have two people groups living side by side. On one side you have Israel, the home of the people of God, Abraham, Isaac, Jacob, King David, and Solomon, as well as it being the location of the great Temple. And then right next door you have this league of ten pagan

---

CHURCHES HAD BEEN PLANTED, DISCIPLES HAD BEEN FORMED, AND CITIES HAD BEEN REACHED BECAUSE JESUS HAD CHOSEN TO GO BEYOND AND REACH THEM.

---

cities ruled by Rome. I discovered that these ten cities were linked by a common culture, a common currency, a common army and a common language. Amazingly, one of these cities was Gadara, which we focused on in our last two chapters.

Historically speaking, if Jesus had been a typical Rabbi, He would not have gone to Decapolis because Decapolis was not a part of Israel. Decapolis was an unclean place. In Decapolis, they partied and got drunk. In Decapolis, they raised and sacrificed pigs to Zeus and the Roman panoply of gods.

Yet the Gospels reveal that Jesus entered Decapolis multiple times. He preached and His fame spread into Decapolis. Decapolis was a mission field for Jesus Christ!

So whatever ended up happening in those filthy, despicable cities? Remarkably, by the Byzantine times, every one of those cities had been reached, and a bishop and an apostolic leadership team had been established in each of the ten cities. Churches had been planted, disciples had been formed, and cities had been reached because Jesus had chosen to go beyond and reach them.

So as I'm getting this word "Decapolis" in my head, I'm asking God, completely perplexed, Why are you talking to me about this? Could it be that you are now intending to extend GateWay's vision into more than these three cities?

The answer was, simply and unequivocally, "Yes". That is when I knew that God was clearly calling us to become one church in multiple cities. We had been faithful in "a very small thing" and the Lord was asking us to "take authority in ten cities".

3 THINGS "DECAPOLIS" MEANS FOR US

DECAPOLIS: A PLACE OF HUGE SPIRITUAL NEED

In Mark 4, we read how Jesus healed the sick, broken, and tormented people of Decapolis. This is more than just a historical account. It is a story of people, like you and me, whose lives were broken and who were touched by Jesus.

ARE YOU EXPERIENCING DIFFICULTY IN YOUR OWN LIFE? JESUS IS THE ONE WHO HELPS BY RELEASING HIS POWER.

Then in the seventh chapter of Mark, we read that Jesus came out from the region of Tyre and through Sidon "into the region of the ten cities" (Mark 7:31).

Remember, this is Jesus, a nice Jewish boy visiting pagan cities! Has he ended up in the wrong neighborhood? No, it was a result of the Holy Spirit leading Him directly there. Here he does one of His most exciting miracles. Mark 7:32–35 (NASB) states,

> They brought to Him one who was deaf and spoke with difficulty, and they implored Him to lay His hand on him. Jesus took him aside from the crowd, by himself, and put His fingers into his ears, and after spitting, He touched his tongue with the saliva; and looking up to heaven with a deep sigh, He said to him, "Ephphatha!" that is, "Be opened!" And his ears were opened, and the impediment of his tongue was removed, and he began speaking plainly.

Miracles took place in Decapolis!

Are you experiencing difficulty in your own life? Jesus is the One who helps by releasing his power.

I also want you to understand that if those of you, as believers and followers of Jesus Christ, are sometimes encountering difficult circumstances, how much more consumed in brokenness are those in dark, oppressed cities? People are in difficulty in our world today, and it is not as though the world is getting easier; in fact, the condition of our world is getting far worse, but I believe God is going to answer the crisis of our day with a massive revival—a powerful move of His Holy Spirit—where countless people are going to come to Christ.

I am going to prophesy. I see thousands of churches that will be planted by many movements like us. Brand new pastors, elders, and intercessors are going to be raised up, and we will see cities change by the power of God! This will happen in the United States just as it did in Decapolis—a place of huge spiritual need like our own, a place where miracles occurred, and a place where Jesus touched the brokenness and the pain of people's lives.

In the Biblical parable about the prodigal son (Luke 15:11–32), the son left his father's house, choosing instead to travel to a distant land seeking pleasure. What kind of a land did that end up being? Well, the son lost all his money partying, quickly finding himself as a servant feeding pigs. When he decided to come home, covered in shame and regret, it was only a day or two journey for him to return.

I can't prove this theory, but I believe when Jesus created the parable of the prodigal son, He was talking about being in the faraway land of Decapolis. There was an abundance of pigs, parties, and paralyzing emptiness. And Jesus ended the story by illustrating how, in the fullness of time, the Holy Spirit touches a person's heart, bringing him back to the father's house and leaving the broken places behind. Surely this inspires us to believe that God loves such places and is at work in the lives of those there in sin.

DECAPOLIS: A HARVEST OF SOULS
For me, Decapolis is about more than a region—it symbolizes opportunity. It's not just a broken, sad place, but it is a place where the ministry of Jesus took off!

What happened to these cities when Jesus visited? They received Him and the good news that He brought. They responded to the Gospel, as He knew they would.

After setting him free, Jesus told the demoniac at Gadara to "Go home to your friends, and tell them what great things the Lord has done for you, and how He has had compassion on you." (Mark 5:19) The story goes on to reveal the supernatural harvest of souls in Decapolis because of his obedience: "And he departed and began to proclaim in Decapolis all that Jesus had done for him; and all marveled." (v.20)

When I say Decapolis, I want you to think about a place not only of great spiritual need but also a place where people respond to the Good News.

The city-wide harvest that occurred in Decapolis was a result of somebody going beyond their normal world, experiences, and expectations. Jesus had to leave the comfort zone of Israel and go to the Gentiles. He went to broken, pagan cities because He had a purpose in His heart.

Why should we think about other cities? Why should we make their problems our problems? Let me say this: people are waiting for you and me to become what God has called us to be. People in dark cities, people in places that have never heard of Christ, are waiting for us. Let's go beyond one city just as Jesus did.

THE CITY-WIDE HARVEST THAT OCCURRED IN DECAPOLIS WAS A RESULT OF SOMEBODY GOING BEYOND THEIR NORMAL WORLD, EXPERIENCES, AND EXPECTATIONS.

DECAPOLIS: A PLACE OF DISCIPLESHIP

The people of the Ten Cities became fully committed followers of Jesus Christ. It says He healed them, and "great multitudes began to follow Him." That, my friends, is the essence of discipleship.

The people Jesus healed and preached to in these dark lands started following Him, acting like Jesus, learning about Jesus, and teaching others to do the same until those ten cities of Decapolis had all been reached. This was a true discipleship movement. This is how Jesus transforms cities!

When I think about our call to reach ten cities, I have to ask myself, Lord is it possible that people sitting here in our church could become the pastors, elders, worship leaders, and intercessors of a ten-city apostolic movement? Not for just this church, and not just for our other GateWay campuses. Could it be that there are even more places where, through this network of connection and Kingdom culture, this one heart and one vision could spread out and touch ten cities?

I also wonder, does the word of Decapolis put upon my heart and mind infer exactly ten cities? I don't know for sure what it means, but I sure plan to find out! I just know that God is putting these cities that are beyond our comfort zones upon our hearts, and I believe that He wants us to care about them.

**JESUS IS LOOKING AT THE DECAPOLIS
OF OUR CULTURE RIGHT NOW.**

CONCLUSION

When we think about Decapolis, I would like us to consider the brokenness, hurt, and pain of lost cities. You or I may not know exactly to which city we will be called, but we know there's pain out there, and that is where we want to be and what we want to touch.

I believe that Jesus is looking at the Decapolis of our culture right now. I think He is looking intently upon the people who are broken and lost. And if He's thinking about it, then I want to think about it.

Jesus set the example for us when He went beyond the borders of Israel and thought outside the box. He went where hurting people were. Is there room in your life to be a part of reaching out to more than one city? I believe God wants us to really stretch our hearts and faith out wherever He will lead us, if we will be obedient and do as Jesus did.

Since that day in May of 2016, it has become clear to me that God is calling us to be one church in multiple cities. Let's go beyond just a few cities. Let's reach out as far as God's heart extends.

GOD'S HEART FOR CITIES

In Luke 19, Jesus spoke through the parable of the faithful steward about what He does with and for faithful people. When He gives people something small and they're faithful with it, then He rewards them and increases it for them. The message from Jesus for us remains that we should not be thinking about the things we don't have. Instead, we can think about the things we do have and decide to be faithful with those things, because when we are, God will bless us, increasing us and trusting us with more.

If we want to be promoted to greater things, we need to come back to those little things that are in our hands right now and be faithful with those. If you're playing drums for church, praise God by being a faithful drummer! If you serve as an usher or a greeter, be faithful in those things you are doing for God. Show up on time, do it with all your heart, be faithful, and watch what God will do for you. Perhaps now is the time to challenge yourself by beginning to think about how you can be better prepared for a place in the mighty opportunities God is raising up through the church. Think about attending our school of ministry or some other class or seminar offered within your church or neighboring churches. All of this is part of being actively faithful with what God has provided for you.

I personally cannot escape the power of these words: Because you have been faithful in a very small matter you will have authority in ten cities.

Jesus said in the Great Commission that He wanted His followers to "go into all the world and preach the Gospel" (Matthew 28:19), and I believe the principle of growing influence is crucial. According to His command, we must go into all the world and multiply and be fruitful. Because of this, we know that God must have an enormous heart for cities.

BECAUSE YOU HAVE BEEN FAITHFUL IN A VERY SMALL MATTER YOU WILL HAVE AUTHORITY IN TEN CITIES.

GOD GIVES US AUTHORITY

I shared in the last chapter about my spiritual encounter with the word Decapolis, meaning "ten cities". Remember that Decapolis was a place where there was a tremendous harvest of souls and a great response to Jesus' ministry. With a great discipleship movement born as a result of Jesus' presence, many thousands of people came to faith when He visited those ten cities. This is an inspiration for us today as one church in multiple locations.

God says, "I want you to not just think about your own city as you have been, but now begin to think about other cities." (Luke 19:17) In this way, I believe God is giving us authority. That might sound somewhat pretentious, but it's not. We're not looking to "take over" cities per se. Rather, we want to be a positive influence and see God move to reach the lost.

In the natural sense, the idea of authority in multiple cities is intimidating. I have admitted to God, "Lord, I feel like my plate is full and I don't know how to do this. Are You sure You've got the right guy?"

As an answer to my worries, I felt like the Lord reminded me of these verses in 2 Corinthians 3:2-6. It is here the Apostle Paul states, "It is not that we are competent in ourselves to claim anything as coming from ourselves, but our adequacy is from God" (CSB).

This verse reminds us that God makes us capable as ministers of a new covenant, not of the letter but of the Holy Spirit. It is the Holy Spirit that is going to do the work, not us. We are not adequate of ourselves, nor are we anybody special. The truth is our knees are knocking, and yet we're choosing to say, "Lord, if you're calling us to do this, we're going to trust in you."

This is where we are led to remember the truth of Philippians 4:13, where Paul encouraged us with these words: "I can do all things through Christ who strengthens me" (NKJV).

YOU MAY NOT FEEL AN ADEQUATE MATCH TO YOUR CHALLENGES IN LIFE, BUT JESUS IS!

YOU CAN DO ALL THINGS

While I've talked a little bit about our mission as a church, let me now make this personal: how does this all work for you?

Maybe you're leading a blended family, or you've just started your own business. Maybe you'd like to build a family but you're having challenges. Perhaps you'd like to buy a home, or take a step to improve your education or increase your wealth. Whatever it may be, remember that while you may not be competent in and of yourself, you can do all things through Christ. You may not feel an adequate match to your challenges in life, but Jesus is! God uses weak and imperfect people to do great things.

The Bible says God has chosen the foolish and the weak to confound the wise, so when something does succeed, everybody looks at the situation and says, "That is clearly the hand of the Lord."

When I feel inadequate to fulfill God's vision, I must remember to say, "Lord, I'm ready for you to use me! Even a broken, unlikely person like me! I will put my trust in you, God, and believe you can use me to make something great happen."

Take hold of that for yourself and believe that God can use you right where you are. You can father your children! You can love a woman! You can build a business! You can earn a degree. You can do it! Not in your own power but through the power that comes from the Holy Spirit.

We can do all things through Christ who strengthens us. We can even touch a city through the power of Christ.

IF WE UNITE FOR A HOLY PURPOSE, GOD WILL GIVE US THE ABILITY TO DO GREAT THINGS.

GOD LOVES CITIES

In case we are tempted to consider this outreach to cities unimportant, we should be aware that three out of every four people alive on planet earth today live in cities. Given this ratio, if God doesn't love cities, then most of us are in a lot of trouble! Thankfully, we know that in fact He does love and have a plan for cities, and He wants to work mightily in and throughout them.

In GateWay's effort to reach cities, we're not just tackling practical issues like hunger and homelessness; we're also tackling spiritual problems and family problems. In order to do that we're going to have to work together as a team. One person alone can't do a whole lot, but when people come together there is undeniable power. If we unite for a holy purpose, God will give us the ability to do great things.

When faced with the question of how we as a church are going to be able to affect multiple cities, we encounter many challenging thoughts. How many campus pastors would we need? How many worship teams would we need? How many youth pastors and children workers, how many intercessors, ushers, and elders would we need to see this vision become reality?

None of this makes a whole lot of sense unless God loves cities. And that's the truth we must always come back to: God has a huge heart for and about cities. The Bible emphasizes this fact in Psalms 107:6-7 where it states that, "In their misery they cried out to the Lord, and He saved them from their troubles. He led them on a straight road to a city where they could live" (ICB). This verse communicates the truth that God brings people to cities for the purpose of blessing them.

Many say, "I've got to get out of the city! Cities are terrible! Cities are full of poverty, crime, and traffic jams."

I understand those feelings. But God created cities. He loves them! The reason there are cities to begin with is because God knows we need each other.

We would also be wise to consider what God's idea might have been in creating and encouraging the growth of cities. I believe God says, "I want to bring together places in the earth where people come into community and they help each other, where they have hospitals, churches, educational institutions, and other places where people's lives can get better." This was His intent in creating cities.

So, if cities were God's idea, then we can't give up on them! And we certainly don't want to condemn cities. Sometimes Christians project a lot of Old Testament ideas about bringing fire and brimstone down on cities. For instance, people have been prophesying to us in California for years that our state is going to fall off into the ocean because we're as wicked as Sodom and Gomorrah.

I disagree. I think God actually loves California! I've got a lot of friends and relatives here who love Jesus, and we're definitely not going into the ocean to die. There are righteous people in our cities, and we know undeniably from His word that God loves all people. God loves cities, and He leads people into cities in order to bless and heal them.

GOD WANTS US TO LOVE CITIES

Remember the story of Jonah? He was the guy whom God asked to preach life-saving redemption to a lost city. God said to Jonah, "I want you to go to Nineveh, a wicked city, and tell them about My mercy and My love."

But Jonah was none too pleased with this command. He replied, "I don't like Ninevites; they're pagan people, and their city is wicked."

GOD ISN'T HAPPY WITH US WHEN HE INSTRUCTS US TO REACH PEOPLE AND INSTEAD WE CHOOSE TO RUN.

If you spend some time exploring the story of Jonah, it becomes apparent that Jonah exhibited the qualities of a racist. Go back and study the contextual history, and you'll rapidly uncover his true feelings towards the Ninevites.

So, Jonah boarded a boat going the opposite direction of Nineveh. That's about the time when Jonah came face-to-gill with a rather large fish. A rebellious, racist preacher was in big trouble.

God wasn't happy with Jonah's decision to run. Similarly, God isn't happy with us when He instructs us to reach people and instead we choose to run. When we disobey, God has a way of bringing us back to our callings and assignments.

When Jonah finally submitted to God and got himself to Nineveh, he actually did a great job preaching to the city. But, all the while, he had this lingering attitude in his heart. He gave God's message to the people, but he still did not love the city. He had an attitude, a chip on his shoulder. Even so, the whole city came to faith. They all repented to God of their sins in a city-wide revival.

When this happened, Jonah's reaction was not good. He was very angry with God and complained, "I knew that you were a God of love and kindness! I knew that if I shared your message with these people that they would get right with you. And now you're actually going to save them! Instead of judging them and destroying this city, you're going to bless this city, and God, I'm not happy about it."

But God had a wise and gentle answer for Jonah which reveals the attitude He wants us to carry toward cities: "Nineveh has more than 120,000 people living in spiritual darkness. Shouldn't I feel sorry for such a great city?" (Jonah 4:10).

In other words, God was saying to Jonah, "I love this city, but you hate this city. There are 120,000 people here that are in spiritual darkness. Where is your love for this city?"

The grammar of this phrase in Hebrew, "Shouldn't I feel sorry for such a great city?", translates more accurately as, "Should I not weep for this city?"

I think the Holy Spirit would ask a similar question of you and I today. Are we weeping for our city? Or, are we trying to get out of our city? Maybe you even have feelings of hatred and disdain for the people of your city. But God has a different idea. He cries out to us, "I want you to love your city."

WHEN GOD LOOKS AT A CITY, HE LOVES IT AND WEEPS OVER IT.

The story of Jonah says that God loved Nineveh enough to weep over it. The Bible tells us Jesus also wept over a city. Remember in Luke 19 where Jesus wept over Jerusalem?

When God looks at a city, He loves it and weeps over it. He sends us to help cities, not to abandon them or despise them. Loving cities should be at the heart of our mission as churches.

GOD WANTS US TO IDENTIFY WITH CITIES

"...Seek the peace and the prosperity of the city to which I have carried you in exile. Bless the city, pray for the city and seek the peace of the city..." Jeremiah 29:7 (NIV)

In the context of Jeremiah 29, the children of Israel had been carried out of their homeland into the pagan city of Babylon. Considered the worst city in the world, we still regard the name Babylon as synonymous with sin. The children of Israel were dragged from Jerusalem into this evil city as captives. They were now slaves.

In response to their calls of distress, God instructs them, "Plant vineyards, settle down, marry. Don't try to escape; you are going to be here for a while. Seek the peace of this city, and pray for it."

God told them to settle down and settle in. Get connected. Identify with the city. Stop trying to live so separate that you don't talk to people, connect to people, or take time to love people.

Years ago, I had a life-altering personal experience with this exact imperative from God. In 1988, my wife, Kathy, and I had moved out of our area when we were called to be missionaries in the Philippine Islands. Just after we sold our home to make the big move, the biggest real estate boom in local history occurred in Santa Clara County. In the short timeframe that we were working in the mission field, the home that we had just sold had more than doubled in price.

Not too long after we had left, our church called us back from overseas to return to San Jose. We packed up from the Philippines, came home, and we rolled up our sleeves and began working here in our church.

Now the kind of home we needed was completely out of our reach financially. We were forced to live in a small condo on the wrong side of town. For seven years, Kathy and I cried out, "Lord, we had a home! We went to serve You like You asked, and now we don't have a good place to live. We're in this cramped condo and our kids have to play in a backyard the size of a doormat. God, how are we going to be able to afford a home again?"

One Sunday morning in 1995, the sun was shining brightly as I was driving up Highway 101 across the Highway 280 overpass to get to our church in Willow Glen. Suddenly the presence of the Lord came and filled my car. I was looking at the skyline of our city from the overpass, and I felt the Holy Spirit whisper this question to me: Do you love this city? Are you asking for a house just because you want a house, or are you willing to actually make a commitment to this city?

Instantly, I felt convicted. God was asking, "Are you going to unpack and make this city your city? Because if this is your city, I'll give you a home in it." I thought about this, and I responded, "Lord I will commit to this city."

THE LORD WANTS US TO LOVE AND IDENTIFY WITH CITIES JUST AS HE DOES.

I've centered my life in the city of San Jose ever since, and I am heart deep in this place. This is my city, and I love it. And do you know what God did for us? In 1997, within one short year of my commitment to love my city, God did a total miracle in our lives and opened a door for us. We moved into a larger home through supernatural circumstances, and I believe it was because I finally chose to unpack my bags and love my city.

The Lord wants us to love and identify with cities just as He does. When we do, He will do amazing things.

GOD WANTS US TO REACH CITIES

For this last point, allow me to bring us back to the Land of the Gadarenes. After that tormented mean was set completely free by Jesus, he was given an assignment that reflects Christ's heart for cities:

> As he was getting into the boat the man who had been de-mon-possessed asked if he could go with him. But Jesus did not permit him to do so. Instead, he said to him, "Go to your home and to your people and tell them what the Lord has done for you, that he had mercy on you." So he went away and began to PROCLAIM in the DECAPOLIS what Jesus had done for him, and all were amazed."
> Mark 5:18–20 (NET, emphasis mine)

Jesus told him, "If you want to do something for me out of gratitude, go to the ten cities." He had a heart to reach cities that were ripe for the harvest. This is the heart of Jesus for cities, and it is what drives our vision for Ten Cities.

Paul and the early apostles also saw that the Lord wants cities reached. They were able to turn the Roman Empire upside down because they concentrated their work in cities. Why did they focus on Corinth, Ephesus, Rome? They understood that cities were strategic. They knew that if you reached cities, you reached the world.

The best way to reach a city is for us to follow Jesus together. Think about His approach to cities: He went to an earthly city, and he wept over it. He identified with its people. He preached the gospel in that city, and he sacrificed himself for it. In doing that, he has built for us a city with foundations whose builder and architect is God.

It's all about cities! And Scripture records that God has a city planned for us in eternity:

> "I saw a new heaven and a new earth, for the first heaven and the first earth had passed away...I saw the Holy City, the new Jerusalem, coming down out of heaven from God..." Revelation 21:1-2 (NIV)

Do you see it? You too can be part of Christ's eternal plan for reaching cities by going into an earthly city, weeping over it, identifying with it, preaching to it, and sacrificing for it. Are you ready to join Jesus' work in cities?

ARE YOU READY TO JOIN JESUS' WORK IN CITIES?

CONCLUSION

The time to love and reach cities is now. Life is brief, and someday we are going to stand before the Lord and give an account to Him. Personally, I want to be able to say to the Lord, "I had a little bit, and I was faithful with it." I hope your prayer today is something like, "Lord, I want to take the little bit I have and I want you to use me."

If you want to get connected to a vision to reach people, you've got to have a heart for cities. You have to love cities the way God loves them. You have to identify with cities and see God's eternal purpose in them. Join me in this vision to reach ten cities. It will take all of us faithfully using our God-given gifts to bring Him glory in the cities that He loves so much.

BEGGING FOR THE BODY OF CHRIST

If we are to go beyond our comfort zones and embrace the call to reach cities, we need to develop a love for the body of Christ and a passion for prayer. Short of that, we will never unlock our destiny. In this chapter, our journey takes us into the moments after Jesus had died and before He rose again, into the world of a man called Joseph of Arimathea. Here we will learn the secrets of begging for the body of Christ.[4]

> *"Now when evening had come, there came a rich man from Arimathea named Joseph who himself had also become a disciple of Jesus. This man went to Pilate and he asked for the body of Jesus. Then Pilate commanded the body to be given to him. When Joseph had taken the body, he wrapped it in a clean linen cloth and laid it in his new tomb which he had hewn out of rock and he rolled a large stone against the door of the tomb and he departed."*
> *Matthew 27: 57-60 (CEB)*

---

4. This chapter was inspired by a profound message that Pastor Jentezen Franklin preached at the 2016 Conference of ARC (Association of Related Churches) in Birmingham, AL. I gratefully acknowledge his insight.

Out of an incomprehensible love for you and I, Jesus willingly surrendered His life to abuse and death, being beaten, tried, and falsely convicted. He was spit upon, jeered at, jabbed, poked, whipped, and tortured. His body was made a horrific mess.

On the brink of death, Jesus gasped, "...Father, forgive them, for they know not what they do..." (Luke 23:34, KJV). Uttering his final words, He sighed, "...Father, into your hand I commit my spirit!..." (Luke 23:46, AMP).

The Bible explains that it was at this point that Jesus actually offered up His spirit, fulfilling a promise He had made at an earlier time: "No one takes [my life] from me, but I lay it down of my own accord..." (John 10:18, ESV). And so there Jesus was, fulfilling His own words, as well as dozens of Hebrew Scriptures, when He surrendered His spirit through death.

While His abused body was being removed from the cross by the Roman soldiers, one man, Joseph of Arimathea, entered the scene seeking custody of His remains. This Joseph and his bid to take loving custody of Christ's body can have a profound impact on the way we view the church as the Body of Christ.

JOSEPH FOUND HIMSELF ENTERING INTO AN UNBELIEVABLE OPPORTUNITY TO PLEAD FOR THE BODY OF CHRIST.

JOSEPH OF ARIMATHEA

So, who was Joseph of Arimathea? Prosperity had given him great fame and a high social standing. Notably, he was also a member of the Sanhedrin, which was a type of Jewish Supreme Court. All of this made Joseph of Arimathea a well-known man in his city.

In the book of Matthew, it explains that Joseph was also a man of faith and a disciple; he was a follower of Jesus Christ. The Gospel of Mark informs us that he was actively looking for the Messiah. Luke, too, reveals that during the unfair condemnation of Jesus during His trial, Joseph of Arimathea was one of the few Sanhedrin members not consenting to His death. He did not want any part of the proceedings and was in no way in agreement with what was taking place. But even through this heartrending set of circumstances, Joseph found himself entering into an unbelievable opportunity to plead for the body of Christ.

Joseph of Arimathea's wealth and prestige opened a door for him, putting him before the Roman governor Pontius Pilate at a time when few others could have an audience with a man of such power. This was his opportunity to make a bold request regarding the recently crucified body of Jesus. He had a tomb—a new and expensive tomb that he had hewn out of stone. The Bible tells us that his tomb was located in a garden just outside the city, close to a rock known as "Golgotha" where Jesus had been crucified. It was also here that Joseph's tomb was located, and it was his decision that this tomb be used to shelter the broken, bleeding, and abused body of Jesus.

The Bible says that Joseph of Arimathea begged for the body of Christ (Matt. 27:58). He begged for the opportunity to be involved with the Body of Christ. How he loved the body of Christ!

THE BODY OF CHRIST

What does the story of Joseph of Arimathea have to do with our goal of impacting cities? The Bible reveals that the church is the Body of Christ (Ephesians 5:23, Colossians 1:24). We have a clear mission to reach people, and now, God is giving us even more vision for cities beyond our own. As the church (the Body of Christ), we are called to plant new locations of the Body of Christ in new cities.

HOW PASSIONATE IS OUR COMMITMENT TO GET INVOLVED IN THE BODY OF CHRIST?

So the fundamental question is, how passionate is our commitment to get involved in the Body of Christ? Are we as passionate as Joseph of Arimathea who, with all his money, wealth, and reputation, identified with this broken, bloody mess that was the body of Jesus?

I believe that, as a follower of Jesus, Joseph anticipated the Resurrection. But, for the moment, he came as an intercessor before the Roman governor and communicated his heart's desire: "Please let me position the Body of Christ for a miracle! Let us not allow the Body of Christ to rot. Let us not give way to the birds, that they may pick at the Body of Christ. Let's not allow His body to suffer neglect. Instead, let us steward it into a place where it can await the Resurrection God has promised."

It is as if Joseph is proclaiming, "Yes, I am a man of wealth, and I've got everything, but I'm going to lay it all on the line right now! I care about the Body of Christ. Your men crucified Him, but He's precious to me, and I'm not ashamed to be associated with Him. I have a room for Him." This brand of commitment and passion for the church is essential to our success.

HOW TO BE AN INTERCESSOR FOR CITIES

Joseph of Arimathea is the stellar example of an intercessor, and oh, how I pray that God will grip our hearts as individuals and as churches to also intercede for the Body of Christ. Let me share with you three things about how one individual can become an intercessor in his or her city:

COMPASSION FOR THE BODY OF CHRIST

It all begins with compassion, like Joseph of Arimathea had for the Body of Christ. He was deeply moved in his heart, loving Christ's body so much that he couldn't stand the thought of it being neglected. He had a heavy burden for the Body of Christ that urged him to put his reputation on the line.

By doing as he did, Joseph became like Nehemiah, who also presented himself before a powerful authority figure. In the Old Testament, Nehemiah came before a king to cry out for Jerusalem. He had heard that Jerusalem had been reduced to rubble and burned to the ground. Similarly, it is time for us to plead for the church, to care about the work of God, and to have a burden and a passion for the work God wants to do through us.

Personally, I am on fire to see the Body of Christ built up. I have a desire to see God move through you and me as never before. I do not despise the Body of Christ, and I am not ashamed of the Body of Christ. I'm not ready to say that it is just a broken mess, that it's dead, or that the best days of the church are over. That is simply not true.

Recently, I read the words of a particularly honest young person on Facebook—a millennial that ranted passionately regarding her shame of Evangelical Christianity and the church. As I have what I consider a "front row seat" to the weaknesses of the Body of Christ, I really can understand the mistakes and fumbles the church makes.

Yet, I wonder if this young lady will have much in common with Joseph of Arimathea when she meets him in heaven. As a believer, she wants nothing to do with the Body of Christ. How might Joseph of Arimathea see it? I believe he would say something like, "I know this body is bloody; I know it's broken. I know it looks dead, but where are the people that will plead for the body? Where are the people that have a burden to care for the body?"

The apostle Paul believed the body of Christ was special and holy. He deeply loved the church. He defended it, warning, "Watch out for the wolves! Don't let anybody come in here and attack the church" (Acts 19:28-31). His entire life was a statement of love for the church: "I'll fight for the church, I'll raise funds for the church, I'll travel for the church, I'll go to jail for the church! I will be beaten for the church, because the church is the Body of Christ."

The difference between the perspectives of my friend on Facebook and those of Paul and Joseph of Arimathea is simple: as broken as the body of Christ clearly was, Joseph knew what the Father knew: a resurrection was coming. It would happen in the very same tomb that housed this broken body. That broken mess was going to turn into a glorious body that would become the Bride of Christ—a living expression of His ministry here on the earth.

A burden for the church is foundational to our mission of touching cities and nations. It is the Body of Christ that is going to accomplish this. Therefore, the church needs people who have the heart of an intercessor, who, like Joseph of Arimathea, will say, "I am crying out for the Body! I see its brokenness, but I'm not giving up on the Body."

THAT BROKEN MESS WAS GOING TO TURN INTO A GLORIOUS BODY THAT WOULD BECOME THE BRIDE OF CHRIST—A LIVING EXPRESSION OF HIS MINISTRY HERE ON THE EARTH.

COVERING THE BODY OF CHRIST

In taking custody of Christ's Body, Joseph of Arimathea also covered it.

While modest, every picture that you may have seen of Jesus hanging on the cross is inaccurate. You see, He did not enjoy have the benefit of a loin cloth. The Romans gave him no such courtesy. Part of the humiliating experience integral to crucifixion was being stripped naked and put on full display in your own city. Being paraded around naked, spit upon, mocked and cursed in your own home-town before dying a slow, vicious death on a cross was all part of the pure terrorism of crucifixion. This deathly act was intended to humiliate everyone involved.

When Joseph of Arimathea took pity on the body, it was completely naked. What do you suppose was the first thing he wanted to do when the body was in his possession? He obtained a cloth and said, "Let's cover Him." The broken and uncovered state of the body was not going to become a morbid spectacle.

His example points us to the heart of intercession—covering the Body of Christ. 1 Peter 4:8 offers us a poignant lesson about the protective nature of love when it says that, above all, we must love each other deeply, because "love covers".

This is counter-cultural in a society that is addicted to criticism. We are often so self-entitled, all we want to do is pass judgment on everything we experience. Every dish of food, every person who speaks, every politician is subject to our incessant evaluations. We pick at our kids, our leaders, and each other. When a person has a flaw, it becomes fodder for delicious gossip. We pass around story after story to morbidly uncover the nakedness of another person.

That isn't love. It isn't kindness or honor.

What kind of churches are we going to have, and what kind of people are we going to be? Are we going to be intercessors, or will we be accusers?

What do you do with the imperfections of the people in your life? Will you rip the covers off and make sure everybody sees, or are you going to be like Joseph of Arimathea, choosing to cover them?

Proverbs says this: "One who seeks love conceals an offense" (Proverbs 17:9, CEB). Have you been offended recently? Perhaps you, like I, have been tempted to gossip about a person's sin, thinking, "It's so delicious, I just need to pass it along...it's more of a prayer request, really." In these moments, we must remember that accusers expose, but intercessors cover.

ARE WE GOING TO BE INTERCESSORS, OR WILL WE BE ACCUSERS?

Noah was an imperfect man. He had too much wine, took his clothes off, and fell asleep. When his sons discovered his state, they walked backwards toward him with a blanket to cover the nakedness of their father. They honored him as a servant of God. Likewise, if we're going to take cities and touch lives, we must be intercessors who will cover, with honor and love, the Body of Christ.

CREATING SPACE FOR THE BODY OF CHRIST
The third reason I love Joseph of Arimathea is because he created space for the body of Christ. He had dug a new tomb out of sheer rock, and this he surrendered to a holy purpose. It was a space that, once given to God, became the site of a resurrection miracle.

When you and I surrender the valuable space in our lives, in our schedules, in our budgets, in our thoughts, and in our prayers for the use of the Body of Christ, miracles happen. Resurrection always comes to the space we dedicate to Him.

As Christians, we need to say, "I'm going to try to carve into my life a place of prayer and fellowship and communion with God. I'm going to make time to read my Bible. I'm going to teach my children to make space on Sunday for the Body of Christ, coming together to worship and to celebrate."

I pray that you carve out a place about which you can say, "God, here's what I have. It wasn't easy. It was a lot of hard work to create this place, but now I turn it over to you.

While I am not a legalistic person, I do fear that the cares of the world could choke out the life of God in us, just as Jesus warned. Things such as a career, sports, and life's pleasures are not inherently evil. I pray God lets you enjoy all those things. But none of them should take the place of God.

I always find it mystifying that the more people's lives and families are falling apart, the less time they have for God. Out of love, I must warn you to keep space in your life for Jesus and the Body of Christ. That's where your miracle is and where resurrection power comes.

As I stated earlier, I am not ashamed of the Body of Christ, and I have chosen to make the time to be in God's house and to connect in a small group of people. Maybe you don't have much time, but you do have some time you can carve out to give to God, saying in faith, "This is where a resurrection could take place."

YOUR PRAYERS CREATE A PLACE FOR GOD.

Your prayers create a place for God. Your local church giving also carves out a place for Him. The reality is, we're not going to take cities with good intentions alone. It's going to be the result of prayer and of hard work, and it's going to be because people are giving and making a space in their lives.

I'm not talking about being in church seven nights a week or some other kind of crazy, unbalanced commitment. I want you to enjoy your life; in fact, I bless you to enjoy your life. But if you are enjoying life so much that the God-space in your life is getting smaller and smaller, I say to you, you are going in the wrong direction.

I challenge you that it might be time for you to get the chisel out to your budget, to your schedule, and even to your children's and spouse's expectations. Maybe now is the time that you're going to knock out some space in your family's world for a miracle. Make room for the Body of Christ, for fellowship, for Bible reading, and especially for spending time with Jesus.

CONCLUSION

Ask yourself today, do you have space in your life for the Body of Christ? Do you love the Body of Christ, and will you cover the Body of Christ? If you do, you are an intercessor that God can use to affect entire cities.

RELATIONSHIPS THAT REACH CITIES

If I were to ask you what the greatest moments in your life have been, how would you answer? You could probably think of some real mountain-top moments, like your wedding day or the birth of your child. And what if I were then to ask you about the most painful, difficult times in your life? What hurt you the most and really brought you down?

Chances are the answer to both questions involved relationships. In fact, I'm betting the aspect that made these events so great or so painful was probably something going on in a relationship, because our relationships determine so much about our lives.

As we approach this chapter, I want to zero in on this idea of relationships from the city-reaching perspective. Let's discuss the question of whether or not God's call on our lives requires us to be involved in relationships. In an effort to get at our answer, let us begin by peering into the life of the early church.

THE EARLY CHURCH: OUR RELATIONAL EXAMPLE

What kind of relationships did the early Christians have—these individuals who were the first ones to come to know Christ during the first days of the church? What were their lifestyles like regarding relationships? Let's see if we can find some clues about relationships in the early church as seen in Acts 2:

They continued steadfastly in the apostles' doctrine and fellowship in the breaking of bread and in prayers. Then fear came upon every soul, and many wonders and signs were done through the apostles. Now all who believed were together, and had all things in common, and sold their possessions and goods and divided them among all, as anyone had need. So continuing daily with one accord (that's also relationship language), continuing daily in the temple and breaking bread from house to house, they ate their food with gladness and simplicity of heart, praising God and having favor with all the people. And the Lord added to the church daily those who were being saved. Acts 2:42–47 (KJV)

**GOD IS CALLING US TO BE A PART OF
RELATIONSHIPS THAT REACH PEOPLE.**

Notice all the relational language here: "All things in common," and "in one accord." The early followers of Jesus took good care of each other, and the church grew daily. There was a clear reason for the impressive momentum that the early church possessed of so many people coming to Christ on a constant basis. It was their relationships.

I believe God is calling us to engage in new kinds of relationships—relationships that become instrumental in bringing others to Jesus. God is calling us to be a part of relationships that reach people.

I often look back on how it was that my wife and I were saved in our teenage years. We were rebellious teenagers, doing all kinds of things young people definitely should not be doing. Neither of us lay the blame on our parents for our choices because we both had great parents! The truth is that though we knew better, we were choosing to live the wrong kind of lives.

There was an incredible emptiness and hunger in us. This deep longing was affecting our generation by the tens of thousands. People in their teens and twenties started coming to Jesus in floods. It was a time of revival that to this day is remembered as "The Jesus Movement." It was during this unique and dynamic time that Kathy and I came to the Lord.

What made that movement so strong and lasting had a lot to do with relationships. There were such deep friendships and strong connections. Everything happened to us together as we grew in the Lord and grew in our faith. While we were getting to know Jesus better, we learned to pray, to be married, and to be young leaders. We didn't have a clue what to do next, but we were together! All the milestones in our lives were profoundly affected by our relationships with each other. Our emotional and spiritual growth was not so much a result of classes we took or degrees we attained. It was our friends and spiritual leaders that we connected with who taught us how to live for the Lord.

Building healthy relationships is crucial in each of our lives, because at the end of the day it isn't the books you read or the sermons you hear that enhance your life and ministry—it's the people you know who help you and actually do life with you.

In Acts 6, we discover that the message of God was moving powerfully and spreading like wildfire. The early church was increasing and the number of disciples was multiplying (v.7). It began in the city of Jerusalem but soon extended to other cities. Even the Jewish priests within the city became followers of Jesus.

How did something so miraculous happen? What was going on? This all occurred because of their strong relationships. It was as though people were pulled together en masse into Christianity because of the connections they had with each other.

By the time we get to Acts, chapter 9, thousands in the church throughout all of Judea, Galilee, and Samaria were being built up and filled with great peace (v. 31). People were getting stronger, growing, and walking in the fear of the Lord. The power of the Holy Spirit was causing the church to transition from simple addition to magnificent multiplication.

The early church is a picture of what the modern church is supposed to be. Their relationships with each other literally changed world history.

It is relationships that give us spiritual reach. God wants to release tremendous power through us in our communities, but just like an electrical system, if we don't have the correct wires connecting (meaning we don't have our relationships right with each other) then the power just isn't able to flow.

**THE POWER OF THE HOLY SPIRIT WAS CAUSING
THE CHURCH TO TRANSITION FROM SIMPLE ADDITION
TO MAGNIFICENT MULTIPLICATION.**

If you have wondered, "How can I grow closer to God? How can I mature spiritually and emotionally?", the answer is better relationships. "How do I get more joy and power in my life?" You get more joy and more spiritual power through better relationships. Relationships will touch every area of your life, simultaneously making our churches better, stronger, and more capable of reaching cities.

THREE RELATIONSHIPS THAT REACH

There are three types of relationships that I see within the early church that helped them to reach people and touch cities:

THEY HAD A CLOSE RELATIONSHIP WITH THE LORD.

The people of the early church had a genuine and intense relationship with God. They were a praying church that entered into God's presence together. They experienced praise and worship as they were singing about all that Christ had done. And while they did so, the glory of God came to fruition through signs and wonders and miracles. Clearly, this was not a dead religion but a living relationship.

Remember the cultural context of the early church. There was a strong religious culture in the city of Jerusalem. Recall also that Jesus was a Jewish man in a Jewish city with the Jewish temple and its priests. All the priests were dressed in their specified uniforms, and they performed their pre-established and time-honored rituals. An important reason behind the priestly rituals was that they were done to make sure that people's sins would be taken away through offerings and sacrifices. It was an ancient and highly-respected system.

While I have no desire to be critical of their culture, it should be recognized as a religious system and structure that was strong within that city. All of that structure existed so that people could relate to God. Unfortunately, it was a distant relationship with God; all contact with Him was made only through the priests. You would give them your offering and sacrifices, so that they could present it to God. Then they would come back to essentially let you know, "God says you're okay." It was an arm's-length transaction with God, performed through the priesthood.

WE NOW HAVE DIRECT ACCESS TO A RELATIONSHIP WITH GOD THROUGH FAITH.

But all of that became unnecessary because Jesus Christ became the perfect Lamb of God. He became our righteousness on the cross, and we don't need a priest to intercede for us anymore! We now have direct access to a relationship with God through faith. This is what Paul was explaining in the book of Romans, chapter 5, when he wrote that we are "have access to God's grace by faith" (vv. 1–3). Our justification is no longer accomplished by way of a priest. It's not your offering that gets you straight with God! It's your faith. And Paul said that it is through this faith we find peace with God.

Do you have that kind of peace with God? It's a beautiful peace that only comes from a close, personal relationship with Him. By faith in Jesus, we can have an intimate connection with God. We no longer need priests or rituals.

The good news of the Gospel is that it's not hard to have a relationship with God because of what Jesus has done. When He died on the cross for our sins, that barrier between us and Him was taken away, and if we have faith, then we can know Him. It's just that simple. And an authentic relationship with God is the key to all of life.

THEY HAD CLOSE RELATIONSHIPS WITH THEIR
SPIRITUAL LEADERS

We've just seen how complicated the Jewish system was and how the Jewish priests did all the talking to God for the people as their spiritual mediators. There's an additional contrast to make, which is that the Jewish system also had a kind of a spiritual hierarchy. Only certain people from specifically outlined backgrounds could be priests.

Though this was normal for their time and culture, once again the cross of Jesus changed everything. As Christians, we no longer operate under a hierarchy. Yes, we still do have leaders within the church, but the relationships that we have with our spiritual leaders (pastors, teachers, and so forth) is not supposed to be distant or hierarchical, but close and interactive. In reality, however, this is not always the case.

As a church leader, I often joke with people by saying things like, "You don't want me coming to your birthday party because when I come into the room, everybody straightens up. It's as though I'm an alien from another planet!" But I promise you and everyone else: I have the same problems and fears you do. I'm just a normal person, only with a leadership position in the Body of Christ. I'm trying to be faithful to the Lord within this calling, but in the end, leaders are just people!

How did we all become so disconnected from our spiritual leaders? There is too much fear and apprehension about relating to them.

In the early church, it wasn't that way. In fact, they were close to their leaders. The early church had leaders that loved and were for the people, teaching and training them as they fed the people with the Word of God. Some of those leaders were called apostles, and they were anointed with the Holy

---

I BELIEVE IT IS TIME WE TAKE CONNECTING WITH OUR LEADERS MORE SERIOUSLY.

Spirit's power and given the grace to lead people into blessing. Acts 2 says the people responded to such men by devoting themselves to the apostles' teachings. In other words, the people were waiting to hear what they should do and how they should live, and they were truly excited about what their leaders were saying to them. This is a closeness that is very important to have in the church, and yet I think that type of relationship is exactly what is missing from so many churches. I believe it is time we take connecting with our leaders more seriously.

In Ephesians 4:11, Paul talks about Jesus calling individuals to roles of importance and usefulness within the church, stating, "And He personally gave some to be apostles, some prophets, some evangelists, some pastors and teachers, for the training of the saints in the work of ministry, to build up the body of Christ..." (HCSB).

Leaders are a gift from Christ to us. Understanding this is powerful. If we actually value the gift God has given to us through His appointed leaders, the result is akin to the ferocity of a powder keg ready to explode.

Predictably, it is within this type of positive relational setting that the enemy comes in to put a wedge in our relationships. He wants to put a stop to that growth and cast a shadow of doubt among us. He doesn't want relationships to do their powerful work in the earth.

Leaders are imperfect, and they make mistakes. This sometimes leads to people being hurt, and it is that hurt which blocks people off from their leaders.

Sometimes being in a close relationship hurts. It's the same as in marriage. I ask husbands all the time, "Do you love your wife?"

They (hopefully) respond, "Yes, I do!"

"Well, do you ever hurt her?"

"Yes."

"Did you mean to?"

"Uh..., well, no."

Don't throw your relationships away because they sometimes hurt. Work through the pain and keep the relationships when you can.

GateWay is a growing church, and I love to meet the new people we have coming in and out of our doors every week. Occasionally when I meet people that have come to us from other churches, I learn that there was a problem in their past with a leader at a church. What I take from this is that it could happen here in my own church, just as it could happen in any church. Situations such as these can cause people to choose to remain in church but avoid a leader.

Now, if you were the devil wouldn't you just love to see that happen? If the hurt or offense in a person's life has blocked them from having a great relationship with a leader, the enemy has won, and it will be hard to reach cities.

Let me make this personal. If I, or any pastors or leaders have done anything to hurt and disappoint you, on behalf of whoever it was, I ask that you would please forgive us. Don't let that

BE OPEN TO HAVING RELATIONSHIPS WITH THE LEADERS THAT GOD HAS PUT IN YOUR LIFE.

be the cause of a painful break in your fellowship. There is too much at stake. Additionally, I would ask you, if somebody from another church has upset or hurt you, please forgive them. Please let them go. Release them and keep growing in your relationship with God. Be open to having relationships with the leaders that God has put in your life. Hebrews 12:15 reminds us that we have to watch out for these hurts: "Being careful lest anyone fall short of the grace of God; lest any root of bitterness springing up trouble you..." (KJV).

What is bitterness? Think about the shelf life of milk. It's good one day, but at some point you smell it and it's foul. Similarly, your hurts have a shelf life. You only have a certain amount of time to fix a hurt before it really starts to sour you. And if you don't attend to it, it inevitably will change you.

You fix this problem through forgiving and choosing to work on giving that pain to God. So many people have been through divorces, break-ups in the business world, or have broken up with their pastors, or their friends, and experienced death in all kinds of relationships.

My challenge to you is that there's a shelf life on that pain, so do not let it fester! How do people get angry and nasty? I believe it is because they have allowed too much pain to build up on the inside, and it ends up changing who they are. Beloved, this is not what Christian people should do! We are called to forgive. We must forgive, we must let go, and we must bless. The only thing that's going to change a city, a marriage, or a family is a transformed and forgiving heart.

If we are going to reach cities for Christ, we need to be like the early church—close to God, close to their leaders, and close to one another.

THEY HAD A CLOSE RELATIONSHIP WITH EACH OTHER

The early church had strong connections with each other. Acts 2 says they were, "Possessing all things in common." They were together in one accord, and they took care of each other as they connected in the temple. They conducted their large gatherings much like we do church on Sundays, but they also met house to house. In that way, they actually did life together.

What is it that is going to reveal to the world who Jesus really is? Jesus said in John 13:35 that "Your love for one another will prove to the world that you are my followers" (NLT). It will be our love for one another that proves our genuine devotion to Christ.

You see, Jesus changes everything. He restructures our relationships and unites us so we can we do life together. We should be gathering all the time, seven days a week! Because we are a community, we don't just come together for a service. We should be doing life together. This is about relationships on an intense level of authentic community.

GateWay is a place like this. We love each other. Today, I'm issuing you an invitation: I'm welcoming you into this relational community of believers. If you come to church once a month, I'll be happy. If you come twice a month, I'll be happier. If you come three times a month, I'll be very happy. But if you start doing life with your church community, I will know that we have the power to reach people in every city we touch.

I'M WELCOMING YOU INTO THIS RELATIONAL COMMUNITY OF BELIEVERS.

CONCLUSION

What we have seen in the passages of Acts about the early churches is that they had relationships that reached people. The early church was a moving force on the earth, and it all began in a city.

When Jesus instructed the disciples, "Go into the city", His heart for cities became evident. He further stated, "Wait there in the city until the power of the Holy Spirit touches you." As they followed His instructions, the power of God touched them. Something entered into their lives that was heavenly, and it wasn't just the overwhelming presence of the Holy Spirit; a deep and authentic sense of community also developed. Their relationships empowered them to reach cities.

In a church like ours, everybody matters. Everybody is important, and love is the main thing. The bottom line is that our relationships really determine our impact on cities, so let us put the focus on relationships. Let's get good at knowing God, knowing our leaders, and knowing each other. Let us draw close to one another and watch how the Lord will take us beyond all limitations together for His glory.

DAVID CANNISTRACI

QUESTIONS AND ANSWERS ABOUT OUR TEN CITIES VISION

To discover more about our vision to reach cities and how you can join the effort, please read the FAQs below. They are organized into the following categories:

- The history, vision, and culture of GateWay City Church
- The practical side of being one church in multiple locations
- The cities we want to reach
- The addition of new locations

The last section is perhaps the most important. Please carefully read the questions and answers about how you can get involved with the vision. Finding your place in God's Kingdom will be one of the most important steps you will ever take.

If you have any additional questions, we welcome you to contact any of our campus pastors at the GateWay location nearest you, or email us at info@gatewaycitychurch.org.

QUESTIONS ABOUT THE HISTORY, VISION, AND CULTURE OF GATEWAY CITY CHURCH

WHAT IS THE HISTORY OF GATEWAY CITY CHURCH?

Our journey began in 1970 in Sunnyvale, when God called Pastors Emanuele and Shirley Cannistraci to lead our church, then known as Calvary Gospel Temple. We were a small group of about 60 members at that time, but God had much bigger plans. Within a few short years, our membership swelled to over 150. Young people were being saved and added to the church during an era of revival now known as the Jesus Movement.

In 1977 God provided a new location in Mountain View, and our church was renamed Church of the Crossroads. Three years later, we sold this property and moved, completely debt-free, into our Willow Glen location. Our church was renamed Evangel Christian Fellowship in the Spring of 1980.

Throughout the 80s and 90s, as our church continued to grow, families were sent as local missionaries, staff and ministries added, programs expanded, and related churches were planted. We have been blessed by a strong history of financial integrity and moral consistency in our staff and leadership team.

In September of 2000, Pastors David and Kathy Cannistraci were installed as the Lead Pastors of Evangel. Pastor David's heart for expansion, ministry development, and creating an outreach culture resulted in further growth, and it soon became clear that our church facility was inadequate.

After a long property search and several attempts to relocate, our church purchased its present facility in South San Jose and changed our name to GateWay City Church. Over the past decade, GateWay has experienced continuous growth. In late 2014, we became a multisite church, and in 2016 we developed a vision to reach ten cities through this multisite strategy.

HOW DID GATEWAY GET ITS NAME?

Our name came about in 2003 when we were relocating to a larger facility. We were facing tremendous disappointments. Financial pressures were growing and our hopes of finding adequate facilities were fading. At one particularly discouraging moment in this process, God clearly spoke to Pastor David about how He would make a "gateway of hope in the valley of trouble" (Hosea 2:15, NLT). Instantly hope was renewed and shortly afterward, we moved into our present facility—one twice the size of what we had foreseen as possible! The words "city church" were also prophetically significant: we would be a church that would reach cities. Our name reflects God's faithfulness, power, and purpose for our ministry.

WHAT IS THE VISION OF GATEWAY CITY CHURCH?

Below you will find a simple but meaningful statement of our vision in ministry. It includes an overview of our ministry culture, purpose, and process. Because our vision involves making disciples, we have developed a set of measurable outcomes that point us to a clear picture of what a disciple looks like.

OUR CULTURE:
Inspiring Transformed Lives

OUR PURPOSE:
- To love and honor God
- To live in wholeness and freedom
- To embrace our God-designed identity
- To influence our culture and community

OUR PROCESS:
Gather, Grow, Go

It is our goal and passion to see all our GateWay family members grow and become strong in four major areas:

1. Loving and honoring God

We want our members to experience a vibrant prayer life and learn to apply God's word to their daily lives. Through building healthy relationships, learning the blessing of a giving life, and sharing the gospel with those around them, members can thrive in our local church, serving God from a place of rest and peace.

2. Living in wholeness and freedom

A central focus of the good news Jesus Christ came to bring is restoration—healing and wholeness for the whole person. We have a passion to see people develop a positive self-image and learn to overcome the negative culture around them. The ability to forgive, to have hope and faith for the future, and to thrive in the context of God-ordained intimacy is evidence of a life of freedom in Christ that we want everyone to experience.

3. Embracing our God-designed identity

God has made each of us unique—our gifts, talents, and abilities suit us to the calling God has for us. We want our members to love the way God designed them to be and to live out of the fullness of their own distinct identities. Then they will be able to relate to others at home, at work, at school, and in their community in a healthy way.

4. Influencing our culture and community

One of our primary focuses as a church is to help each of our members engage with and influence our community and culture with the saving grace of Jesus Christ. We want to reach out with compassion to the hurting and wounded people around us and commit to making disciples and increasing God's kingdom presence in the earth.

The future of GateWay is as bright as the promises of God. Our hearts are filled with faith to fulfill the vision of Inspiring Transformed Lives.

WHAT ARE SOME OF THE DISTINCT QUALITIES THAT HAVE ALWAYS BEEN A PART OF GATEWAY?

Looking back over the decades of our experience as a church, certain things stand out as our "ministry DNA." These are the things that we hold dear—the things that must always continue to distinguish us as a family.

1. **Prayer and Intercession.** Our church has always been marked by extraordinary prayer. Our people seem to have an unusual appetite for prayer meetings, corporate times of fasting, spiritual warfare, and intercession for regional and national revival. Whether it has been expressed in all-night prayer meetings, Saturday morning prayer, annual weeks of prayer and fasting, prayer teams and conferences, or the prayer lives of our leaders, prayer is in our DNA.

2. **Open Worship.** We have always seen worship as a part of the priesthood of every believer. Our services have always included spontaneous open worship, singing a new song, lifting our hands, waiting, lingering, and letting music and voices flow openly across a well-engaged congregation. This dimension of our worship is an important part of ushering in the presence of God and the freedom of the Holy Spirit. (See Ephesians 5:19 and Colossians 3:16)

3. **The Presence of God.** For as long as our church has been together, people have commented about the strong sense of God's presence they experience in our services and gatherings. This is a wonderful part of "presence churches" like ours. We value the sense of God's nearness and the anointing of the Holy Spirit in our atmosphere. Lingering and soaking in the presence of God is a crucial part of our life together.

4. **Prophetic Ministry.** We strongly believe that God wants to speak to His people when they gather together in worship (Acts 13:1-3). The voice of the Holy Spirit in the church can be released through the spirit of prophecy (Rev. 19:10), the gift of prophecy (1 Corinthians 12 and 14), prophetic or new songs (Revelation 5:8-9 and 14:2-3), and the office of the prophet (Ephesians 4:11). We are a prophetic church.

5. **The Power of Praise.** Throughout the history of both Israel and the early church, fervent praise was a powerful weapon against the enemy (See 2 Chronicles 20 and Acts 16). As a church well-versed in spiritual warfare, we have committed to the importance of Spirit-energized singing, clapping, shouting, and even spontaneous dancing that defeats darkness, shakes strongholds, and opens prison doors.

6. **Developing Young Leaders.** From the earliest days of our church, we have carried a passion for activating, training, and developing the lives of young people. They were not just trained as disciples but as the next generation of leaders, intercessors and worshippers. Many of our present church leaders were developed in character and calling primarily through this house. Our focus has never been holding on to ministry, but raising up the next generation of leaders and sending them into the harvest.

7. **Joyful Teamwork**. Perhaps most importantly, a stream of real relationships and true unity has always flowed in our ministry. Some of our most joyful times took place during meetings, rehearsals, or just relaxing and eating together as friends. Authentic love for God and each other has been the glue that has held us together over time. And that's what it will continue to do as we work together in cities.

8. **Healing and Freedom.** From the early days, our leaders have emphasized the importance of a "full Gospel" message which includes not just salvation and redemption, but deep healing and complete freedom for the believer. With a long commitment to freedom and healing ministries, we've seen amazing results in the lives of thousands of people. Many continue to be helped through our services, conferences, Cleansing Stream Ministries, and now our GateWay Healing Center that offers healing, freedom, and prophetic ministry on a monthly basis.

9. **Evangelism and Community Outreach.** Our Founding Pastor was an evangelist by gifting, and our Lead Pastor was a missionary, so the passion to reach the lost through any means possible has been embedded in our DNA. Outreach is a part of everything we do (see our "Gather, Grow, Go" strategy) from our small groups to our primary ministries to our altar calls in every service: we exist to reach lost people! Another part of this passion is our Gateway Community Outreach which meets practical needs of the local community through education, healing, empowerment, and advocacy.

IS DIVERSITY A PART OF GATEWAY'S FOCUS?

We often refer to our church as "A Church for All People." The church at Antioch was led by a racially and culturally diverse group of people (Acts 13:1). We have a history of rich diversity in our church, including a strong representation of both men and women in leadership roles. Our leadership team has determined that we must be even more intentional about cultural and racial diversity as we expand. GateWay City Church condemns racism, sexism, and racial injustice, and is committed to being a church that reflects the diversity of heaven (Revelation 7:9).

QUESTIONS ABOUT BEING ONE CHURCH IN MULTIPLE LOCATIONS

In May of 2016, the Holy Spirit clearly spoke to our Lead Pastor about taking authority in ten cities (Luke 19:17). He received a prophetic vision of reaching out to lost people in multiple cities as the Lord directed him to the Biblical story of Decapolis. This experience has led us to develop an apostolic model of ministry and a passion to touch multiple cities as one church. The book you hold in your hand explains the heart and soul of this approach.

As a part of this vision, since 2014 GateWay City Church has followed the Lord's direction in becoming one church that meets in multiple locations. We have come to believe that the multisite approach is the best way for our church to fulfill it's calling to reach the lost and establish healthy influence in multiple cities.

HOW SUCCESSFUL ARE MULTISITE CHURCHES?
Over the last two decades, more than 8,000 churches have used this strategy with impressive results. In fact, more than 90% of all multisite churches are successful and experience significant growth in the first couple of years.

WHAT ARE THE ADVANTAGES OF THE MULTISITE MODEL?
First, because multiple sites share common resources, campus pastors and staff are freed to focus on people. Second, the multisite model allows smaller churches to enjoy the resources of a large church while still enjoying the family feeling of a smaller church. Leaders who were once isolated and under-resourced are now brought together as a team with a clear focus and strong relationships. Shared systems and clear approaches to ministry aid isolated ministries and provide

spiritual momentum across locations. It is a beautiful model of New Testament apostolic ministry.

WHAT ARE SOME OF THE UNIQUE FEATURES OF GATEWAY'S APPROACH TO MULTISITE MINISTRY?

There are lots of multisite models out there and each one is different. Some use a "video venue" approach, where the teaching ministry comes from one or two central teachers via video. We have chosen a different approach. We train and use local "live" campus pastors as the primary source of teaching and preaching. We do not see them as facilitators, but as gifted leaders in their own right. We relate to them, support them, train them, and oversee them according to our vision, culture, and spiritual DNA.

Our campus pastors are on our combined speaking team. They create our message content together, and align their ministry as one team speaking the same thing across all our locations. We feel this is the best fit for us and our sense of what God wants to do through us.

WHAT DOES OUR CHURCH GOVERNANCE LOOK LIKE UNDER THIS MODEL?

In our structure, there is one Lead Pastor, one legal board, one eldership across all locations (which our pastors would all be a part of) and one church which meets in multiple locations. Depending on the decisions that need to be made, our leaders use internal and external consultation, prayer, study of God's Word, and especially the leading of the Holy Spirit within our team of servant-leaders to govern.

In terms of management systems and methods, we remain flexible. We know that as we grow, we will adjust our organization to stay healthy and meet the changing needs in each location. We will never step away from the leading of the Holy Spirit, or become ruled by traditions or power-hungry leaders. Our leadership is based on the healthy model we see in the New Testament church, which was apostolically led, prophetically driven, and team focused.

HOW ARE OUR MINISTRIES FUNDED?

Each of our locations operates by faith, based on an established budget that depends on the generosity of the people at that location. Through giving tithes and offerings as a part of their worship, the people of GateWay fund the work of God, and the Lord multiplies it in amazing ways.

WHAT ARE OUR WEEKEND SERVICES LIKE?

Our worship services are contemporary, multi-ethnic, multi-generational, Spirit-filled worship and preaching with an unwavering commitment to the Bible, excellence, and a warm welcome for all people. Our preaching and teaching teams consist of local leaders, with occasional special guests. Periodically our Lead Pastor visits us or ministers to us via prerecorded messages. For a complete layout of GateWay's approach to worship and gatherings, please request a copy of our teaching manual, "GateWay's Worship Culture" (Complete contact information can be found in the back of this book).

WHICH MINISTRIES DO WE ALIGN ACROSS OUR LOCATIONS, AND WHICH ONES ARE LEFT TO THE LOCAL TEAMS?

The process of aligning ministries is progressive. We currently focus on aligning our preaching and teaching, calendars, administration and finances, safety policies, small group materials, discipleship materials, and worship culture. We are working toward a greater alignment in the areas of children's and youth ministry, men and women's ministry, healing ministry, freedom ministry, and outreach ministry. This is a work in process, but we are making good gains.

HOW DO WE STAY CONNECTED TO OUR LOCATIONS?

Multisite ministry at GateWay is all about relationships. Our team of leaders regularly visits all of our locations. Our campus leaders and pastors are equipped and inspired to be more effective though special seminars, video conferencing, regular phone calls, quarterly days together, and annual leadership conferences. These gatherings are filled with laughter, inspiration, prayer, and shared ministry, and the interaction between campuses remains a strong priority.

HOW ARE OUR PASTORS COMPENSATED FOR MINISTRY?

Wherever practical, our campus pastors and some staff members are supported through the giving of the people in their location. Some resources from each location are set aside to assist with the administrative costs of each location, including bookkeeping, insurances, administrative personnel, and other expenses. Pastor David and his pastoral team receive no special compensation for their ministry to the other campuses.

QUESTIONS ABOUT THE ADDITION OF NEW LOCATIONS

HOW DOES GATEWAY CHOOSE A CITY TO GET INVOLVED WITH?

This is purely done by the leading of the Lord. As a prophetic church, we follow the voice of the Holy Spirit and move into the doors He confirms as opening to us (See Acts 13:1-3 and 16:6-10). Over the years, our leaders have had impressions of the Holy Spirit about locations but have also had some surprising open doors that were not previously anticipated. Serving God is always exciting, and our business plan is to follow Him wherever He leads us!

DOES OUR APPROACH TO A PARTICULAR CITY VARY ACCORDING TO THE LOCAL CULTURE, CALLING, AND MAKEUP OF EACH CITY?

Absolutely! Our approach to ministry is designed to be broad enough to work well in any location, but flexible enough to adjust to local factors. God has placed unique identities in cities and groups. Pastor David has written extensively on this topic in his book entitled God's Vision for Your Church. God's unique purpose and calling on various cities and groups requires each GateWay location to be sensitive to those unique factors and to tap into those specific opportunities to maximize the effectiveness of our work.

WILL WE PLANT NEW LOCATIONS IN OTHER CITIES UNTIL WE REACH EXACTLY TEN CITIES?

We are looking to expand the number of our locations based on opportunity, leading of the Lord, and available resources. Our focus has been defined by the Lord as including ten cities (see Matthew 4:25, Mark 5:20 and Luke 19:17), but that number may be more spiritual than literal. In the Bible, the number ten speaks of taking responsibility, and we are committed to being faithful with any number of locations for which the Lord makes us responsible.

IN THE FUTURE, WILL WE PLANT INDEPENDENT CHURCHES, OR JUST ADDITIONAL CAMPUSES?

Over the years, GateWay has planted independent churches. Some of them have been very healthy and continue to thrive; others were not as successful. In almost every case, those that were not successful struggled to find the right DNA, resourcing, and leadership as "independent churches." The result was poor health and decline. While we are very open to planting independent churches if all the conditions are right, GateWay's present focus is planting campuses where the connection, DNA, relationship, and resourcing remains strong.

WHY DO WE SOMETIMES MERGE WITH (OR "ADOPT") CHURCHES THAT ALREADY EXIST?

There are several reasons. Sometimes churches that have a similar calling and spiritual DNA to GateWay need additional help to accomplish their purpose. Sometimes a church like this may have a leadership need, a difficult financial situation, or just a strong desire to connect. In such cases, we pray about joining forces to become one church, believing that we could be far, far more effective in reaching our world together than alone.

HOW DO WE MERGE CHURCHES INTO OUR VISION?

We have done this a few times, and each time it is unique process. In each case, though, we go through a process of prayer, discussion, and assessment. Once the decision to merge is agreed upon by everyone involved, we connect legally and spiritually in such a way that Pastor David becomes the lead pastor of the adopted church. The members of the adopted church are welcomed into covenant relationship with GateWay. The pastors and leaders of the adopted church form our Campus Leadership Team, and the best communicators and shepherds become the Teaching Team for that campus. The campus changes its name to become GateWay City Church, and is referred to, for example, as the Santa Rosa campus of GateWay City Church, the Modesto campus of GateWay City Church, etc. With one vision and one team, we are then one church.

WHAT BLESSINGS COME OUT OF THESE KINDS OF MERGERS?

By joining with GateWay, the adopted churches are better resourced and grow more healthily. Because we are doing church together, no one is ever alone. Local bodies of believers become more financially and spiritually secure. Working under the leadership and covering of Pastor David and his team, the pastors and members become more fruitful than they could by themselves. Additional outreaches are developed to reach the lost, and new impact on the community can begin. Opportunities for people to serve, reach out, and fellowship are greatly expanded, and fresh excitement fills the air as friends both old and new join together.

QUESTIONS ABOUT CONNECTING WITH OUR VISION

As a part of our circle of GateWay family and friends, you are a vital part of this vision. We need your help more than ever to move forward in our mission of reaching people.

WHAT IS TEAM GATEWAY?

Team GateWay is the joyful army of men, women, and young people who volunteer to make the vision of GateWay work. There are hundreds of talented and faithful people who regularly serve at all of our locations as teachers, ushers, sound and media people, intercessors, greeters, security people, youth and children's workers, musicians, worship leaders, and more. The members of Team GateWay are led, inspired, and equipped to function in regular meetings of Team GateWay at each location, along with individual and group meetings scheduled by each specific ministry.

HOW DO I GET STARTED WITH THE TEAM?

By reading this book, you have already taken an important step. It is vital that you understand our vision and DNA. Now we ask you to allow God to connect you to it. Let God place it deeply in your heart. Beyond this, your faithfulness in regular attendance, ministry, prayer, and the giving of tithes and offerings is a powerful way for you to identify with those who have come together to accomplish more for Jesus through GateWay City Church.

WHAT IS GROW TRACKS, AND SHOULD I ATTEND?

Our goal is to help you discover, grow, and step into God's plan and purpose for your life. We have designed Grow Tracks as learning experience with this in mind. At Grow Tracks, our leaders will help you do four important things:

- Discover God's unique purpose for your life

- Learn how a church like ours can help get you equipped to fulfill your mission

- Move toward a better place in your ministry

- Reveal Your SHAPE—the unique personality, gifts, and experiences that suit you for ministry

There are four separate classes that are designed for everyone— new believers in Christ as well as veterans in the faith. These classes are conveniently scheduled and include a free meal, plenty of new friends, and lots of inspiration. You'll be given a free workbook filled with great material to keep and study. There is plenty of time for your questions and help in directing your next steps in the Lord.

Completing Grow Tracks is the perfect way to prepare to be a part of our team. By joining Grow Tracks, you'll be taking the next important step in your journey with us and moving into a future of Inspiring Transformed Lives.

I HAVE SPECIFIC SKILLS IN MINISTRY, BUT I HAVEN'T FOUND MY PLACE. WHAT SHOULD I DO?

First, know that we need you! Our vision can only come to pass as God brings the workers and leaders needed to make it work. Please sit down with a campus pastor and share your story. Tell us about your passion. We will get you connected with the right people, training, and ministry opportunities.

CAN I GET A JOB WORKING AT ONE OF OUR LOCATIONS?

As the growth of each church location allows, both volunteers and paid staff members will be added to oversee areas of ministry like children's ministry, student ministry, worship ministry, and outreach. This is looked at on a case-by-case basis under the direction of Pastor David. We are always looking for great people who know how to serve and work well with others.

WHAT ARE SOME STEPS I CAN TAKE TODAY TO CONNECT WITH THE VISION?

There are three important things we ask everyone connected with our church to do.

- **First, seek God.** Pray against the work of the enemy. Pray for unity and harmony. Pray for the leaders at all our locations. Pray for the open doors and resources to continue to reach people. We can do nothing apart from Jesus and the power of His Spirit.

- **Second, report for duty**. Join us at our regular Team GateWay gatherings. We want you to come, meet our campus pastors and, when available, meet Pastor David. Ask questions, volunteer, and find a place to connect in a small group. Watch for details and opportunities to be a part of the vision!

- **Finally, please support GateWay with your time, tithes, and offerings.** The needs are great, and each of us can contribute to our church's future success.

You are a vital part of this vision to go Beyond. Together we are on a mission to love and honor God, live in wholeness and freedom, embrace our God-designed identities, and influence our culture and communities!

EPILOGUE: WHERE DO WE GO FROM HERE?

"Would you tell me, please, which way I ought to go from here?"
"That depends a good deal on where you
want to get to," said the Cat.
"I don't much care where–" said Alice.
"Then it doesn't matter which way you go," said the Cat.
—Alice's Adventures in Wonderland, Chapter 6

In life and in ministry, it really does matter where we're going.

In this simple book, you and I have begun a spiritual journey together. In a way, we have followed in the steps of our Lord and Savior Jesus Christ. We have gone beyond the comfort of our Capernaum—our usual routines and comfort zones in life—to cross over into the Land of the Gadarenes. Like Jesus, we too have heard a cry for freedom from spiritual oppression and have moved toward the distant shores of lost people and spiritual pain. Most importantly, we have seen hope: hope that the love of Christ can change people's lives, hope that the worst sins can be forgiven, and the deepest darkness can be broken.

But our journey is just beginning. We have much further to go if we are to make an impact in the world and fulfill our calling together. Where we go from here will determine whether we will return to our comfortable points of embarkation or if we will open our eyes to see new horizons beyond where we are. There are cities waiting for us to be who we are called to be—cities filled with hunger, receptivity, and spiritual harvest.

Where do we go from here? Our choice will dictate whether we are disciples of Jesus or occasional fans, leaders or bystanders, and intercessors or accusers. If we have hearts like the Gadarene man—filled with gratitude and a desire to reach others—we will ask for our assignment. We will boldly move forward to claim the cities God is calling us to.

Since our direction determines our destiny, let's consider the following thoughts about where we should go from here:

- **Let's get better.** While I have called on us to cover and love the Body of Christ, I am aware that we are broken and bloody. The church is far from perfect. We are often distracted, insensitive, and ineffective when it comes to the needs around us. We are the Body of Christ, and it's time for a resurrection! GateWay City Church is committed to being better at reaching across economic, cultural, generational, and gender divides. We have embraced the call to get better at loving, reaching, engaging, and truly discipling all people. To take authority in cities, we must be better organized, more connected, more authentic in presenting our message, and more sensitive to needs around us. Some say the church is irrelevant, but I know we can fulfill our indispensable role as the very hands and feet of Jesus if we will stretch ourselves to become better.

- **Let's stay centered on Jesus and the Gospel.** What kind of churches are we hoping to build? Many talk about prophetic churches, revival churches, missional churches, or some other culturally-defined style of church. I have seen some churches that are deeply mystical, some that are Las Vegas-flashy, some that are hipster-trendy, and others that seem to be stuck in the 1970's. The true center of GateWay City Church must never be a style or fad—it must be the Gospel of Jesus Christ. That means everything is about Jesus and His ability to change a life. Everything else is secondary—preferences, styles, and opinions included. "For from HIM and through HIM and to HIM are all things. [For all things originate with Him and come from Him; all things live through Him, and all things center in...Him.] To Him be glory forever!" (Romans 11:36, AMP). In a world of temporary trends, we must remain anchored in the eternal Gospel and the person of Jesus Christ. Everything else is passing.

•   **Let's build a culture of unity, engagement, and maturity.** Everything we do at GateWay City Church is an extension of our clearly stated vision (see page 82). Our vision comes first, ahead of our opinions, preferences, conveniences, or personal ambitions. To be effective as a movement, we must each commit to the three cultural goals presented in Ephesians 4—unity, engagement, and maturity in the local church. If we walk in gentleness, humility, patience, and love (vv.2-4), we will never be divided. If each of us identifies our gifting, is equipped, and then actively engaged in ministry (vv.7-13), we will always be healthy and growing. And if we focus on spiritual and emotional maturity, moving beyond childish instability, selfishness, and spiritual deception, we will reflect the maturity and beauty of Jesus Christ everywhere we go.

•   **Let's make disciples, and let Jesus build the church.** My friend Pastor Steve Murrell leads a family of churches called Victory Churches that number more than 100,000 believers in the Philippines. Steve calls himself "the accidental missionary," but when you see how God has used him and his team to change so many lives all over Asia, you know that his ministry is no accident. Steve is all about the local church being engaged in making disciples. Everyone is being discipled and encouraged to disciple others, and the beauty of this simple commitment is striking, especially when you see the results. Steve jokes about how church leaders often exhaust themselves to build their church but forget that Jesus said HE will build the church (Matthew 16:18). According to Steve, we are simply called to make disciples. If we focus on that, Jesus will build the church.

They say that everyone needs to have a direction in life. In this book, I have described my direction as a leader. I am called to serve Jesus Christ by raising up healthy leaders to lead one church that reaches the lost in multiple cities. I am convinced that the local church is the answer when it is healthy, inspired, and resourced. When the church is the church that we see in Scripture, incredible things take place and history changes. For 2,000 years, families, cities, and nations have been changed by the church, and there is nothing greater that we could be a part of than the focus of Christ's love and activity, His bride—the church. There is nothing else like the church!

The vision of Ten Cities is built on a passion for reaching people by extending the church into the beyond. Are you a giver, an intercessor, a musician, or a helper? There is a place for you in this vision. Do you desire to lead, reach people, teach, and serve? However old or young you are, whatever your story has been, you can get engaged with us. It really does matter where you are going, and I welcome you to join us in the journey of a lifetime.

ABOUT THE AUTHOR

Dr. David Cannistraci is the Lead Pastor of GateWay City Church, a multisite church based in San Jose, California. Having served around the world for over 35 years as a pastor, missionary, author, church planter, community leader, and growth strategist, he is known for building an innovative church, inspiring leaders, and cultivating unity in his city.

David's first book, Apostles and the Emerging Apostolic Movement (Regal) has been widely received as a foundational work on the subject of contemporary apostolic ministry. It has been translated into seven languages. David's second book, God's Vision for Your Church (Regal) explores corporate gifting and God's unique purpose for every church, network, and denomination. His articles have appeared in both Charisma and Ministry Today magazines.

David's earned degrees include a Bachelor of Science from Bethany University, a Master of Divinity from Christian International Graduate School, and a Doctor of Philosophy from California Graduate School of Theology.

David and his wife Kathy have been married and in full-time ministry together since 1982. They live in Morgan Hill, California, where they enjoy an active life with their two sons, two daughters-in-law, and four grandchildren.

Contact David Cannistraci
GateWay City Church
5883 Eden Park Place
San Jose, CA 95138

gatewaycitychurch.org | DavidCannistraci.org
@pastorofgateway

53828325R00061

Made in the USA
San Bernardino, CA
30 September 2017